THE
TEACHER'S BOOK
OF LISTS

THE TEACHER'S BOOK OF LISTS

Sheila Madsen and Bette Gould

Scott, Foresman and Company
Glenview, Illinois
London

1112131415-MAL-919089

ISBN: 0-673-16446-2

CONTENTS

PART 2 SIGNS, SYMBOLS, TELESCOPES, AND T-SQUARES 83

PART 3 PEOPLE AND ANIMALS 119

INTRODUCTION

This book is a collection of lists. Many of the lists such as Compound Words, Prefixes and Suffixes, and Homonyms are directly connected with the basic skills and content of a school program. Other lists were fun for us to make and have interesting possibilities for classroom use. For example, Flip-Flop Words can be part of a vowel sounds unit and Cockney Rhyming Slang can be used with rhyming words activities. Topics for independent study or research can be selected from lists such as, Words from People's Names, Awards to Animals, and Women.

We have provided worksheets and activities to illustrate the variety of tasks that can be developed from lists. Notes preceding the lists give background information or suggest ways to use the lists.

As a result of using this book, we hope your students will become listmakers. Making lists is a great organizing process and the lists themselves can be effective devices for sharing knowledge. As your students make lists, they'll encounter new sources of information and learn how to use them. There may be instances where they will find points of disagreement between sources which will lead them to check additional references in order to come to a decision on which fact to accept. In the course of list making you may find you've temporarily lost a few listmakers as they become involved in an interesting information source or a list item they wish to pursue further. It's the process that counts here, but the products can be pretty interesting too.

To help get your students started, an A–Z Topics List follows. Any one of the topics on this list can be developed into another list (see the Foods list). The A–Z format is one of the easiest to follow in developing a list. One-item lists such as this can be expanded by adding definitions, descriptions, or other information in either phrase, sentence or paragraph form. As you thumb through the book, you'll see other ways lists can be presented: charts, tables, picture lists and category lists.

As teachers we made and referred to lists all the time. David Wallechinsky and Irving Wallace's *The Book of Lists* motivated us to write *The Teacher's Book of Lists* as a reference for teachers. Some of the lists are standard (Presidents of the U.S., Geometric Formulas); some are extended versions of ones we already had (Compound Words, Consonant Blends); and some were developed on the basis of our own needs and interests (99 Things to Graph and Survey, Hues, Blues and Fugues). We assume that you, as teachers, make or accumulate all sorts of lists. If you have any lists or ideas for lists you'd like to see included in a second edition of *The Teacher's Book of Lists*, write to us c/o Scott, Foresman and Company, 1900 East Lake Ave., Glenview, IL 60025.

A-Z TOPICS LIST

A   actors/actresses, adjectives, airports, announcers (news, sports, etc.)

B   bad movies, birds, bones, buildings

C   cars, cheeses, chemicals, cities, countries

D   dances, dangerous things, dinosaurs, disasters, dogs

E   Easter things, egg dishes, energy sources

F   fads, foods, football players, furniture pieces

G   garden flowers, gargantuan things, gems, German things

H   hats, heroes, high places, hobbies, holidays, horses

I   ice cream flavors, illnesses, Indian tribes, insects, instruments, inventions

J   jams and jellies, jingles, jobs, juices, junk foods

K   kids, kings

L   lakes, landforms, languages, long and lean things

M   Mexican foods, monetary units, monsters, mountains, movies

N   names, numbers, nuts

O   Olympic events, things you turn on, onomatopoeic names, outfielders

P   parks, parties, pets, places, politicians

Q   famous quips, T.V. quiz shows

R   railroads, things to read, rivers, rocks, roses

S   seas, sci-fi words, sculptures, spooky places, sports

T   teams, television shows, trees, towers, towns, toys

U   undersea dwellers, ungulates, unsafe things, things that go up and down

V   Van Gogh's paintings, vegetables, vehicles, verbs

W   bodies of water, weather words, worries, writers

X   Xmas words, things that are X-rayed

Y   things that make you yawn, yellow things

Z   zany people, things that zig-zag, things that have a zipper, zoo inhabitants

EAT YOUR WAY THROUGH THE ALPHABET—AN A TO Z LIST OF THINGS TO EAT

Ā   apricot

A   anchovy, artichoke, asparagus, aspic, avocado

B   bacon, bagels, bamboo shoots, bananas, beans, berries, blintzes, bologna, bok choy, bouillon, bread, burritos

hard C   cabbage, canapes, cantaloupe, carrots, cauliflower, caviar, clams, cocoa, corn, crab, cranberries, crepes, curry

soft C   celery, cereal, ceviche, cilantro, cinnamon

D   daikon, dates, dill, doughnuts, duck

Ē   ear of corn, Easter eggs, eel

E   egg flower soup, eggplant, escargot, escarole

F   felafel, figs, filets, fish, fondue, frank-furters, fudge

hard G   garbanzo beans, gobo, goose, gooseberries, grapefruit, grapes, gravy

soft G   ginger, gingerbread

H   hamburgers, hazelnuts, herring, hickory nuts, hominy, honey, horseradish, hot dogs, Hungarian goulash

Ī   ice cream, iced tea

Ĭ   Indian curry

J   jam, jello, jelly, jicama (pronounced *hicama,* could be used under H words)

K   kale, ketchup, kreplach, kugel, kumquats

L   lasagna, lemonade, lemons, lentils, lichee nuts, lima beans, limes, chopped liver, liverwurst, lobster, lollipops

M   macaroni, mango, marshmallows,
     marzipan, muffins, mushrooms, mustard
N   noodles, nuts
Ō   oatmeal, okra, oranges
Ŏ   octopus, olives, omelette
P   papaya, parsley, peanut butter, peanuts,
     peas, pepper, pickles, pineapples, pita
     bread, pizza, potatoes, prunes, pudding,
     pumpkin
Q   quail, quince, quinine water
R   radishes, raisins, rhubarb, rice, rutabagas
S   salami, salt, seaweed, sesame seeds,
     spaghetti, spinach, squash, squid, steak,
     stew, succotash
T   tea, toast, tofu, tomatoes, tortillas,
     tuna, turnips, TV dinner
Ŭ   upset stomach
V   vanilla, vichyssoise, vinegar
W   waffles, walnuts, water chestnuts,
     watercress, watermelon, wild rice,
     won ton
X   extra helping
Y   yam, yeast, yogurt
Z   zucchini

THE
TEACHER'S BOOK
OF LISTS

WATCH YOUR LANGUAGE

one

WHAT'S IN A WORD

COMPOUND WORDS

Here is an easy-to-read collection of compounds found in many word lists and beginning readers.

afternoon	doorway	icebox	schoolhouse
airmail	downstairs	inside	snowball
airplane	downtown	into	snowflake
another	driveway	lighthouse	snowman
anything	everyone	mailbag	somebody
baseball	everywhere	mailbox	someday
birthday	faraway	mailman	someone
blackboard	fireman	maybe	something
bluebird	fireplace	meatballs	sometimes
breakfast	fisherman	moonlight	somewhere
busboy	football	newspaper	spaceman
campfire	footstep	nighttime	starfish
catfish	getaway	nobody	sunflower
chalkboard	goldfish	outside	sunlight
classroom	greenhouse	pancake	treehouse
countdown	headlight	playground	upstairs
daytime	homework	popcorn	uptown
dollhouse	houseboat	sandbox	wallpaper
doorbell	housework	sandpaper	workman

. . . . and some more

airport	earphone	iceberg	pawnshop	tattletale
armchair	earring	Iceland	peanut	teakettle
ashtray	earthquake	kettledrum	pineapple	teapot
basketball	eyebrow	keyboard	pocketbook	teaspoon
bathrobe	fingernail	keyhole	postcard	tenderfoot
bathroom	flashlight	kindergarten	racetrack	textbook
bedspread	footprint	landlady	railroad	thunderbolt
beeswax	forehead	landlord	rainbow	thundercloud
bellhop	freeway	landmark	roadrunner	thunderstorm
billboard	gentleman	landslide	roommate	thunderstruck
blackberry	grapefruit	lifeguard	sailboat	timepiece
blueberry	grasshopper	lipstick	salesperson	tiptoe
bookcase	Greenland	masterpiece	seashell	toothpaste
bookshelf	grownup	mushroom	skateboard	turnpike
breakwater	hairpin	necklace	seaway	underpants
bridegroom	handcuffs	necktie	seaweed	undershirt
bridesmaid	handkerchief	nickname	slowpoke	undertaker
butterfly	headache	nightclub	snapdragon	upset
candlelight	headquarters	nightgown	snowstorm	wastebasket
chairperson	hereinafter	nightmare	steamboat	waterfall
checkmate	heretofore	notebook	stepladder	weekend
chestnut	highway	oatmeal	strawberry	wheelchair
checkout	homesick	offshore	suitcase	whirlpool
dashboard	honeymoon	offspring	sunburn	wildcat
doughnut	hopscotch	outdoors	sunglasses	woodpecker
driftwood	hourglass	overcast	supermarket	yourself
drugstore	housekeeper	passport	surfboard	
earmuff	hubcap	password	swordfish	

Compound Word Activities

1. Classify the words into categories such as people, sports objects, foods, directions, and animals.
2. Illustrate the words.
3. Invent definitions based on the words that make up the compound. (bridesmaid—a woman who washes, cooks, and cleans for a bride)

4. Make new compounds by dividing words and recombining parts to form new words.
   (busboy + doorbell = doorboy, busbell)
5. Write the words that make up the compound.
6. Invent some meaningful three-part compound words and use them in sentences.
   (breakfasttime, airportlane, earphonewire)

SHORT VOWEL/SILENT E PAIRS

Al-ale	mat-mate	con-cone	kit-kite
at-ate	nap-nape	cop-cope	mit-mite
ban-bane	pal-pale	cot-cote	pin-pine
bar-bare	pan-pane	dot-dote	pip-pipe
cam-came	par-pare	glob-globe	quit-quite
can-cane	past-paste	hop-hope	rid-ride
cap-cape	pat-pate	lop-lope	rip-ripe
car-care	plan-plane	mop-mope	shin-shine
dam-dame	rag-rage	not-note	sin-sine
Dan-Dane	rat-rate	pop-pope	sir-sire
fad-fade	sag-sage	rod-rode	sit-site
fat-fate	Sam-same	rot-rote	slid-slide
fir-fire	sat-sate	ton-tone	slim-slime
flak-flake	slat-slate	tot-tote	spit-spite
gag-gage	spat-spate	bid-bide	strip-stripe
gal-gale	stag-stage	bit-bite	Tim-time
gam-game	tam-tame	dim-dime	tin-tine
gap-gape	tap-tape	din-dine	trip-tripe
hat-hate	van-vane	fin-fine	twin-twine
Jan-Jane	wag-wage	grim-grime	win-wine
lam-lame	wan-wane	grip-gripe	cut-cute
mad-made	met-mete	jib-jibe	hug-huge
man-mane	pet-Pete		jut-jute
mar-mare			us-use

From *The Teacher's Book of Lists* © 1979, Goodyear Publishing Company, Inc.

PREFIXES AND SUFFIXES

Definitions for these common prefixes and suffixes have been simplified. Only the most frequently used meanings of the prefixes and suffixes have been selected for the list. The words given as examples generally contain a root word that children can easily identify.

Prefixes

AD-, AC-
1. to, toward: *ad*verb, *ad*equate, *ac*credit, *ac*custom
2. near: *ad*renal

ANTE-
1. before, prior: *ante*date
2. in front of: *ante*chamber, *ante*room

ANTI-
1. against, opposite of, in opposition to: *anti*slavery, *anti*freeze, *anti*climax, *anti*aircraft

BI-
1. two: *bi*cycle, *bi*annual
2. twice during every or once in every two: *bi*weekly, *bi*monthly

CIRCUM-
1. around: *circum*navigate, *circum*lunar

CO-, COM-, CON-
1. with, together: *co*exist, *com*patriot, *con*form

CONTRA-, COUNTER-
1. against, opposite: *contra*diction, *counter*balance, *counter*clockwise

DE-
1. opposite of: *de*code
2. remove from: *de*horn, *de*throne
3. reduce or lower: *de*flate, *de*grade

DEC-, DECA-, DEKA-
1. ten: *dec*ade, *deca*liter

DIS-
1. not, opposite of, reverse: *dis*belief, *dis*orderly, *dis*approve

From *The Teacher's Book of Lists* © 1979, Goodyear Publishing Company, Inc.

2.   apart, away from: *dis*lodge

EN-

1.   put on or into: *en*throne, *en*danger, *en*act

2.   cover or surround: *en*close, *en*wrap, *en*fold, *en*circle, *en*compass, *en*gulf

3.   make: *en*able, *en*large

EX-

1.   former, before: *ex*president

2.   from, out of, beyond: *ex*change, *ex*hale, *ex*port

EXTRA-, EXTRO-

1.   beyond, outside the scope or region of, besides: *extra*sensory, *extra*ordinary, *extro*vert

HYPER-

1.   more than usual, in excess: *hyper*active, *hyper*critical, *hyper*sensitive

HYPO-

1.   under, beneath: *hypo*dermic

IN-, IM-

1.   not, without: *in*active, *im*possible

IN-, INTRA-

1.   in, into, within: *in*born, *intra*spinal

INTER-

1.   jointly, together: *inter*lace, *inter*twine

2.   between or among: *inter*island, *inter*continental

MID-

1.   middle: *mid*way, *mid*town, *mid*term, *mid*summer, *mid*brain, *mid*day

MIS-

1.   wrong, wrongly: *mis*quote, *mis*advise, *mis*copy, *mis*inform, *mis*judge, *mis*read, *mis*pronounce

2.   bad, badly: *mis*fortune, *mis*treat, *mis*adventure, *mis*shapen, *mis*conduct

MONO-
1. one, single: *mono*rail, *mono*tone

NON-
1. not: *non*fiction, *non*-American, *non*conformity, *non*breakable

OUT-
1. greater, better: *out*distance, *out*dance, *out*run, *out*fight, *out*do, *out*live
2. outer place: *out*doors, *out*side, *out*field, *out*post

OVER-
1. beyond, too much: *over*eat, *over*act, *over*heat, *over*ripe, *over*sleep

POST-
1. after, later: *post*war
2. positioned behind: *post*dental

PRE-
1. before or at an earlier time: *pre*school, *pre*historic, *pre*mature
2. in front of: *pre*fix

PRO-
1. for, in favor of: *pro*-American, *pro*-labor

RE-
1. again: *re*do, *re*finish
2. back: *re*turn, *re*bound, *re*call

RETRO-
1. backward: *retro*gress, *retro*active, *retro*rocket

SUB-
1. under: *sub*soil, *sub*way
2. not up to, inadequate, less than: *sub*standard, *sub*normal
3. part of a whole: *sub*station, *sub*culture, *sub*district, *sub*committee

TRANS-
1. move from one place to another: *trans*plant
2. across: *trans*continental, *trans*atlantic, *trans*oceanic
3. change: *trans*form, *trans*figuration

TRI-
1. three: *tri*colored, *tri*lingual, *tri*angle, *tri*motor
2. once in every three: *tri*monthly
3. three times during every: *tri*weekly, *tri*annual

UN-
1. not, opposite of: *un*clean, *un*clear
2. reverse or opposite of an action: *un*button, *un*pack
3. lack of: *un*easy, *un*rest

Suffixes

-ABLE, -BLE, -IBLE
1. able to, capable of, possible to: eras*eable*, reprodu*cible*
2. tending or likely to: peac*eable,* peris*hable*

-AL
1. belonging to, having the characteristics of: musi*cal*, nor*mal*, industri*al*, trib*al*
2. process of action: refus*al*, arriv*al*

-ANCE, -ANCY, -ENCE, -ENCY
1. quality, act, or condition: resist*ance*, assist*ance*, depend*ence,* emerg*ency*

-ANT, -ENT
1. be in or perform a certain act: serv*ant*, deodor*ant*, solv*ent*

-ATE
1. result or act of, provide with: refriger*ate*, hyphen*ate*

-DOM
1. area ruled by: king*dom*
2. condition or state of being: free*dom*, martyr*dom*

From *The Teacher's Book of Lists* © 1979, Goodyear Publishing Company, Inc.

-ESS

1. female: godd*ess*, host*ess* lion*ess*

-EST

1. superlative of adjectives: bigg*est*, slow*est*, small*est*, healthi*est*

-FUL

1. full of: joy*ful*, beauti*ful*
2. character of: shame*ful*, grace*ful*, man*ful*
3. quantity that would fill: cup*ful*

-FY

1. to form into or become: beauti*fy*, classi*fy*, lique*fy*, nulli*fy*, sissi*fy*, solidi*fy*

-HOOD

1. state of being: child*hood*, man*hood*
2. membership in a group: brother*hood*, priest*hood*

-IC

1. pertaining to, of, part of: angel*ic*, alcohol*ic*, volcan*ic*

-ICS

1. art, science, study of: ceram*ics*, systemat*ics*, tact*ics*
2. act or practice of: athlet*ics*, gymnast*ics*

-ISH

1. nationality: Turk*ish*, Scott*ish*
2. likeness to: mann*ish*, clown*ish*, child*ish*
3. somewhat: brown*ish*, warm*ish*, tall*ish*

-IVE

1. having the quality of: mass*ive*
2. tending to: disrupt*ive*, instruct*ive*

-LESS

1. lack of, without: penni*less*, head*less*, shoe*less*, shirt*less*, meat*less*

-LET

1. smallness in size or importance: play*let*, leaf*let*
2. worn on the body: ank*let*

-LIKE

1. similar to: child*like*, life*like*

-LY

1. in a certain manner: sad*ly*, quick*ly*, efficient*ly*

2. like, having a resemblance to: man*ly*, queen*ly*

3. occurring every: year*ly*, month*ly*

4. in a certain place: third*ly*

-MENT

1. result of, thing produced by: engage*ment*, entangle*ment*

2. process or act of: develop*ment*, detach*ment*

3. state, quality, or condition of: amaze*ment*, enjoy*ment*

-NESS

1. manner or state of being: dark*ness*, unhappi*ness*

-OR

1. person or thing that performs: audit*or*, creat*or*, escalat*or*, govern*or*, investigat*or*

2. state, manner, or act: err*or*, pall*or*

-SHIP

1. state of: kin*ship*, friend*ship*

2. office, rank, level: intern*ship*, lord*ship*

3. art or skill: author*ship*, horseman*ship*, marksman*ship*

-TION, -SION

1. action or process of: pronuncia*tion*, rejec*tion*

2. condition: comple*tion*, starva*tion*, confu*sion*

3. result of: discus*sion*, transla*tion*

-TY, -ITY

1. state, quality, or amount: fals*ity*, humid*ity*, safe*ty*, mediocr*ity*, obes*ity*, inferior*ity*

2. 10 times: six*ty*

-WARD, -WARDS

1. toward, in the direction of: back*wards*, north*ward*

-WISE

1. way, direction, or manner: counterclock*wise,* length*wise*

2. in respect to: time*wise,* money*wise*

-Y, -EY

1. characterized by, resembling, having: rain*y*, storm*y*, slim*y*, thirst*y*

2. quality or state of: jealous*y*, victor*y*

3. act, place, or business: baker*y*

4. little or small: bunn*y*, pant*y*

WORDS FROM PEOPLE'S NAMES

Sylvester Graham (1794–1851) advocated a vegetarian diet and other natural foods. His followers ate unleavened biscuits made of whole grain flour that were called graham crackers. Many other words we use have come from people's names. Here are 70 more.

ampere	ferris wheel	marcel	saxophone
babbitt	forsythia	marconigram	sequoia
begonia	fuchsia	masochistic	shrapnel
bloomers	gaillardia	maverick	silhouette
boycott	galvanize	melba toast	spoonerism
boysenberry	gardenia	mercerize	St. Bernard dog
braille	gerrymandering	nicotine	teddy bear
bunsen burner	guillotine	ohm	timothy
camellia	hooligan	pasteurize	titian
cardigan	kaiser	poinsettia	Tommy Atkins
cereal	loganberry	pollyanna	tommy-gun
chauvinist	lothario	pompadour	victorian
daguerrotype	lynch	praline	volt
dahlia	macadam	pullman	watt
diesel engine	machiavellian	quisling	wisteria
doily	mackintosh	raglan	zeppelin
dunce	magnolia	sadist	
fahrenheit	malthusian	sandwich	

LATIN AND GREEK STEMS

Latin Stems

ACT (do, drive)
actor, deactivate, reaction

AQUA (water)
aquarium, aquanaut, aqueduct

AUDI (hear)
audio, audition, audience

CENT (hundred)
centipede, cent, century

CREAT (make)
creation, creative, recreation

DIC, DICT (say, speak, declare)
diction, dictator, indictment, prediction

DUC, DUCT (lead, draw, bring, take)
produce, productive, aqueduct, deduct

EQU (same, even)
equity, equation, equator, unequal, equilateral

FER (carry, bring)
transfer, ferry

FLEX (bend)
flexible, reflection

FRACT (break)
fragile, fragment, fraction, fracture

FUSE (pour)
transfusion, refuse, confused

GRESS (step, go)
progress, aggressive, digress

JECT (throw)
project, inject, subject, eject

LIBER (free)
liberation, liberal, liberty

LOC (place)
location, local, locate

MAL (bad)
malice, malign, malediction

MANU (hand)
manipulate, manuscript, manual, manufacture

MARE (sea)
marine, submarine, maritime aquamarine

MEM (keep in mind)
memory, memorize, remember

MIT (go, send)
remit, transmitter, admit, emit

MOB, MOT, MOV (move, movable)
mobile, motor, promoted, automobile

OCTO (eight)
octave, octet, octagon, octopus, octogenarian

PED (foot)
pedal, pedestal

PEL (push, drive)
propel, expel, repelled

PEND (hang)
append, pendant, dependent, suspend

PLI (fold)
pliable, duplicate, complicate

PORT (carry)
portable, export, report, import

SCRIB, SCRIPT (write)
prescription, postscript, describe

UNI (one, single)
uniform, reunite, unicycle, unity

VAC (empty)
vacate, vacuum, evacuate

VIS (see)
vision, vista, revise, invisible

From *The Teacher's Book of Lists* © 1979, Goodyear Publishing Company, Inc.

Greek Stems

astro (star): astrology, astronomy, astrologer

auto (self): autograph, autobiography, automobile

bio (life, living things): biography, biology, biopsy

geo (earth, land): geography, geometry, geology

gram (something written down, drawn, or recorded): telegram, electrocardiogram

graph (something that writes, written): autograph, photograph, telegraph

gyro, gyr (circle, spiral): gyroscope, gyrate

hemi (half): hemisphere

hydro (water): hydrofoil, hydrogen, hydrophone

meter (measure): speedometer, odometer

micro (small): microscope, microphone, microfilm

mono (single, one): monotone, monograph, monogram

ology, logy (study of, science of): biology, geology, psychology

phone (sound, voice): microphone, telephone, phonograph

photo (light): photograph, phototype

poly (many, much): polyhedron

scope (instrument for seeing or observing): telescope, microscope

sphere (ball, globe): atmosphere, hydrosphere

tele (far away, distant): teletype, television, telegram

therm, thermo (heat): thermometer, thermostat

zoo (animal): zoo, zoology, zoography

WRITE IT RIGHT—HOMONYMS

acclamation, acclimation
adds, ads, adz
aerie, airy
ail, ale
air, ere, err, heir
aisle, I'll, isle
allowed, aloud
altar, alter
ate, eight
auger, augur
auricle, oracle
bail, bale
baize, bays
bald, balled, bawled
balm, bomb
band, banned
bare, bear
based, baste
beat, beet
beer, bier
bell, belle
better, bettor
blew, blue
bloc, block
boar, bore
boarder, border
bough, bow
bouillon, bullion
braise, brays, braze
bridal, bridle

cache, cash
capital, capitol
carat (karat), caret, carrot
cedar, ceder, seeder
cell, sell
cent, scent, sent
cense, cents, scents, sense
cereal, serial
cetaceous, setaceous
cheap, cheep
chews, choose
choler, collar
choral, coral
chorale, corral
chord, cord, cored
chute, shoot
cite, sight, site
clause, claws
coarse, course
coax, Cokes
colonel, kernel
core, corps
cue, queue
cymbal, symbol
dear, deer
dense, dents
descent, dissent
desert, dessert
dew, do, due
die, dye
doe, dough
ducked, duct

ewe, yew, you
faint, feint
fair, fare
faze, phase
feat, feet
fisher, fissure
flair, flare
flea, flee
flew, flu, flue
flocks, phlox
flour, flower
foaled, fold
for, fore, four
foul, fowl
frays, phrase
frees, freeze, frieze
gait, gate
gamble, gambol
genes, jeans
gilt, guilt
gneiss, nice
gnu, knew, new
gored, gourd
grate, great
grease, Greece
groan, grown
grocer, grosser
guessed, guest
guise, guys

From *The Teacher's Book of Lists* © 1979, Goodyear Publishing Company, Inc.

hair, hare
hall, haul
handsome, hansom
hart, heart
hay, hey
heal, heel, he'll
hear, here
heard, herd
higher, hire
him, hymn
hoard, horde
hoarse, horse
hoes, hose
hole, whole
hour, our
humerus, humorous
idle, idol, idyll
in, inn
invade, inveighed
jam, jamb
jinks, jinx
kill, kiln
knave, nave
knead, need
knight, night
knit, nit
knows, noes, nose
lacks, lax
laps, lapse
leak, leek
lessen, lesson
levee, levy
links, lynx
load, lode, lowed

loan, lone
locks, lox
made, maid
magnate, magnet
mail, male
main, Maine, mane
marshall, martial
mean, mien
meat, meet, mete
might, mite
moose, mousse
muscle, mussel
oar, or, ore
one, won
paced, paste
packed, pact
pail, pale
pair, pare, pear
palate, palette, pallet
patience, patients
pause, paws
peace, piece
peal, peel
pearl, purl
pedal, peddle
peer, pier
plait, plate
pore, pour
praise, prays, preys
presence, presents
prince, prints
principal, principle
profit, prophet

quarts, quartz
rain, reign, rein
raise, raze
rapped, rapt, wrapped
read, red
read, reed
real, reel
right, rite, write
ring, wring
road, rode, rowed
roes, rose, rows
rote, wrote
rye, wry
sail, sale
scene, seen
seam, seem
seas, sees, seize
serf, surf
sew, so, sow
shear, sheer
side, sighed
sighs, size
sleight, slight
soar, sore
sole, soul
some, sum
staid, stayed
stair, stare
stake, steak
stationary, stationery
step, steppe
straight, strait

suede, swayed

suite, sweet

sundae, Sunday

tail, tale

taught, taut

team, teem

tear, tier

teas, tease, tees

their, there, they're

threw, through

throes, throws

thyme, time

tic, tick

to, too, two

toad, toed, towed

toe, tow

tracked, tract

undo, undue

vain, vane, vein

wade, weighed

waist, waste

waits, weights

war, wore

ware, wear

weak, week

wood, would

yoke, yolk

Name _____

A HOMONYM GIFT LIST

Directions: Write in a homonym for the underlined word and the name or kind of person who might get the gift.

1. a new boat _sail_ on _sale_ for _Captain Hornblower_

2. a _____ donut with a _hole_ for _____

3. a pretty _____ and a bag of _flour_ for_____

4. _hoes_ and a _____ for _____

5. a night at the _____ _in_ Washington, D.C. for _____

6. every _Sunday_, an ice cream _____ for _____

7. a new _red_ book that can be easily _____ for _____

8. a _____ of music would bring _peace_ to _____

9. a _____ of paint in a _pale_ color for _____

10. _wood_ _____ be good for _____

11. a fishing _reel_ made of _____ steel for _____

12. a _____ about the monkey's _tail_ for _____

13. the _right_ kind of pen to _____ with for_____

14. a sweet-smelling _____ to be _sent_ to _____

15. a _____ of knives to _pare_ a _pear_ for_____

ANTONYMS

abet-hinder
above-below
accept-decline
active-passive
addition-subtraction
adroit-clumsy
advance-retreat
against-for
agree-refuse
allow-forbid
answer-question
appear-vanish
arrive-depart
artificial-real
asleep-awake

beautiful-ugly
beginning-end
big-little
bold-timid
boring-interesting
bottom-top
boy-girl
brave-craven
busy-idle

capture-release
cheap-expensive
clean-dirty
close-distant
closed-open
cold-hot
come-go
compete-cooperate

complex-simple
contract-expand
cooked-raw
cool-warm
crooked-straight
dangerous-safe
dark-light
dawdle-hurry
day-night
death-life
deposit-withdrawal
division-multiplication
down-up
dry-wet
dull-shiny

eager-reluctant
early-late
east-west
easy-difficult
empty-full
entrance-exit
evening-morning
extinguish-ignite
failure-success
false-true
far-near
fast-slow
fat-thin
female-male
few-many
fierce-gentle
finish-start

first-last
flexible-rigid
follow-lead
foolish-wise
forget-remember
found-lost
fragile-tough
freeze-melt
freezing-sweltering
fresh-stale

guilty-innocent
halt-proceed
happy-sad
hard-soft
hate-love
heavy-light
high-low
hit-miss
horizontal-vertical

in-out
left-right
lengthen-shorten
less-more
long-short
loser-winner
loss-gain
loud-soft
maximum-minimum
most-least
new-old
no-yes

noisy-quiet
north-south
occupied-vacant
off-on
ordinary-strange
over-under

plentiful-scarce
polite-rude
poor-rich
private-public
problem-solution
pull-push

rough-smooth

short-tall
shout-whisper
sick-well
sit-stand
start-stop
strong-weak

tame-wild
thick-thin

Antonym Activities

1. Make a list of synonyms for each word in the pair of antonyms. Example:

   BEGINNING   — start, origin, preface

   END   — finish, terminal, terminate, complete

2. Use a pair of antonyms in the same sentence.

   I arrived *early* at school, but was *late* coming home.

   The *crooked* path led to a *straight* road.

3. Make antonym steps by starting a new pair of antonyms with the last word of the preceding pair.

   stop-start

      start-finish

        finish-begin

          begin-end

            end-opening

              opening-closing

Name _____

ANTONYM ALBUM

Look at the pictures on this album page. Label each picture with a pair of antonyms.

From *The Teacher's Book of Lists* © 1979, Goodyear Publishing Company, Inc.

CONSONANT BLENDS/DIGRAPHS

These words have been arranged so that short-vowel words are listed first.

BL	**BR**	**CL**	**CR**
blink	brat	clap	crack
blast	breath	clement	crest
bless	brig	clip	crib
blunt	brought	clod	crop
blotter	brunt	closet	crumb
bleed	brave	club	crazy
blow	breed	clay	creed
blame	bright	clean	crime
blind	broken	climb	croak
	brood	cloak	crew
	brown	clue	crawl
		clout	crowd

block

blanket

blender

bread

branch

bridge

brush

broom

claw

clock

cloud

crab

cradle

crayon

cross

cry

DR	**FL**	**FR**	**GL**
drab	flat	fragment	glad
drift	flesh	fresh	glen
dread	fling	friend	glisten
drawl	flop	frill	glob
droop	flutter	frost	glutton
drake	flake	frustrate	glade
dream	flea	freight	glee
drive	flier	freeze	glide
drone	float	fry	glow
drew	fluke	frozen	glue
drought	flour	frugal	gloom

drip

flag

frog

gloves

dress

fly

frown

dropper

flame

fruit

drum

flower

From *The Teacher's Book of Lists* © 1979, Goodyear Publishing Company, Inc.

GR	**PL**	**PR**	**SC, SK**
gratis	plank	practice	scamp
grid	plastic	press	scat
grovel	pledge	prison	scare
grip	plod	principal	scope
grate	pluck	prod	scold
grease	plunder	pray	scowl
grind	play	preen	skim
groan	plead	pride	skin
group	please	probe	skip
groom	ply	prune	skeleton
growl	Pluto	prowl	skeptical
	ploy	proof	

grass

grapes

plaid

plate

plow

present

scarf

ski

skates

skunk

skull

SL

slam
slept
slit
slot
slumber
slate
sleep
slice
slope
sloop

sled

slide

slippers

slacks

SM

smash
smack
smell
Smith
small
smog
smug
smear
smooth

smile

smoke

SN

snag
snip
snuff
snuggle
sneak
snide
snoop
snout
snare

snail

snap

snore

SP

spank
spatter
sped
spill
Sputnik
spunk
space
speak
spy
spore
spew
spoil

spear

spider

spool

spoon

spot

From *The Teacher's Book of Lists* © 1979, Goodyear Publishing Company, Inc.

ST	SW	TR	TW
staff	swam	traffic	twist
stab	swell	trap	twinkle
standard	swift	trend	twitch
steps	swim	tread	twill
stick	sway	trinket	twain
stock	sweet	trip	tweed
stumble	swipe	trod	tweak
stare	swollen	tropical	tweet
steel	swoon	trump	twice
style	swoop	trust	twine
stole		trail	
student		treat	
stoop		tribe	
		troll	
		true	
		trouble	
		trout	

sweater

swan

stop sign

swing

train

QU

quarrel
question
quickly
quit
quake
quite
quote

queen

quail

SPL

splash
splendid
split
splint
splotch
spleen
splice
splurge

splinter

SCR

scrap
scramble
scrimmage
script
scrub
scrape
screen
scream
scribe

scroll

screw

SPR

spread
sprig
sprinkle
sprocket
sprung
sprain
spray
spree
spritely
spry

spring

SQU	STR	CH	SH
squander	strap	chatter	shadow
squiggle	strength	checkers	shed
squint	strip	chip	ship
squish	strong	chop	shock
squeeze	struggle	chuckle	shut
	strum	cheap	shade
	stray	chime	sheen
	stream	choke	shine
	strike	choose	show
	stroll	chew	shoot
	strew	chocolate	shawl
			shelf

squid

square

squirrel

strawberry

string

straw

street

stripe

chain

cherries

chipmunk

children

church

check

shell

shark

sheep

shamrock

TH (unvoiced)	TH (voiced)	WH	SHR
thatch	that	when	shrank
thin	them	whether	shrapnel
think	then	which	shred
thunder	there	where	shrill
thought	they	whine	shrink
thief		white	shrub

thumb

thimble

thermometer

whistle

whiskers

whale

wheel

whip

shrimp

From *The Teacher's Book of Lists* © 1979, Goodyear Publishing Company, Inc.

WORD ENDINGS

-FT	**-MP**	**-ND**	**-NG**
craft	champ	band	bang
cleft	cramp	land	sting
drift	ramp	sand	string
sift	hemp	wind	long
soft	limp	kind	wrong
tuft	romp	pound	hung
	dump	round	lung
	hump		

raft

lamp

wand

ring

chimp

pond

king

shrimp

wing

-NK	**-NT**	**-SK**	**-SP**
tank	slant	flask	asp
spank	bent	task	rasp
link	hint	risk	clasp
shrink	tint	whisk	grasp
honk	front	husk	crisp
chunk	hunt	tusk	
junk	runt	kiosk	

sink

tent

mask

skunk

plant

desk

trunk

paint

present

From *The Teacher's Book of Lists* © 1979, Goodyear Publishing Company, Inc.

-ST	**-CH**	**-SH**	**-TH**
last	crunch	crash	bath
best	teach	flesh	path
mist	coach	mesh	breath
cost	porch	wish	tenth
rust	couch	gosh	month
waist	ouch	crush	faith
least	staunch	rush	tooth
coast		wash	truth
roost			uncouth

fist

wrist

church

peach

fish

dish

mouth

teeth

VOWEL DIGRAPH AND DIPHTHONG WORDS

Digraphs

ai as in sail	ay as in day	ea as in team	ea as in head	ea as in break
afraid	clay	cream	bread	steak
aim	crayon	deal	feather	
chain	gray	easy	heather	
fail	lay	flea	lead	
jail	may	gleam	measure	
maize	play	grease	read	
paid	prayer	leak	tread	
paint	slay	mean	treasure	
praise	stay	peak	weather	
proclaim	sway	plead		
rain	tray	preach		
snail		repeal		
stain		seam		
straight		squeal		
train		teach		

ee as in week	ei as in eight	ey as in key	ie as in piece	oa as in boat
flee	freight	donkey	belief	coat
free	neigh	honey	chief	float
glee	neighbor	monkey	lien	load
green	rein	trolley	relief	moat
heed	skein	volley		poach
need	sleigh			road
queen	vein			roam
seed				soak
sheen				toad
sheet				
sneeze				
steed				
sweet				
three				
tree				

oo as in foot	oo as in moon	ow as in crow	ue as in blue
book	balloon	blow	due
cook	bassoon	flow	glue
crook	croon	low	gruesome
good	fool	mow	sue
hood	hoot	row	true
look	room	slow	
shook	school	throw	
stood	shoot	tow	
took	spoon		
wood	stool		
	swoon		
	too		
	tool		
	toot		
	zoo		

Digraphs followed by r

air as in pair	ear as in year	ear as in earth	ear as in bear	eer as in deer
eclair	appear	Earl	pear	beer
fair	beard	early	tear	cheer
flair	clear	earn	swear	leer
hair	dear	heard	wear	peer
lair	dreary	hearse		queer
stair	ear	learn		seer
	fear	pearl		sheer
	gear	search		steer
	hear			
	near			
	rear			
	spear			
	tear			

ier as in pier	oar as in oar	our as in four
fierce	boar	pour
pierce	roar	
tier	soar	

Diphthongs

au as in taught	aw as in saw	ew as in grew	oi as in oil	ou as in out
caught	crawl	blew	avoid	blouse
flaunt	draw	crew	coil	cloud
haul	drawl	dew	coin	couch
haunt	fawn	drew	foil	foul
maul	gawk	flew	hoist	house
pauper	hawk	new	join	loud
sausage	law	slew	loin	mouth
taut	lawn	stew	loiter	mouse
	raw	threw	noise	ouch
	shawl		point	pouch
	straw		poison	pound
	tawny		soil	round
	yawn		spoil	shout
			toil	south
			voice	trout

ow as in cow	oy as in boy
down	coy
drown	destroy
flower	employ
fowl	enjoy
frown	joy
gown	ploy
how	Roy
plow	toy
renown	voyage
shower	
town	
trowel	

From *The Teacher's Book of Lists* © 1979, Goodyear Publishing Company, Inc.

SILENTS, PLEASE—COMMON SILENT LETTERS

silent gh	gn, silent g	kn, silent k	wr, silent w	mb, silent b
bought	gnarl	knack	wrap	bomb
caught	gnash	knapsack	wreath	climb
dough	gnat	knave	wreck	comb
eight	gnaw	knead	wren	crumb
flight	gneiss	knee	wrench	jamb
high	gnome	knew	wrestle	lamb
right	gnu	knife	wring	limb
sleigh	align	knight	wrinkle	numb
sigh	arraign	knit	wrist	thumb
taught	feign	knob	write	tomb
thought	reign	knock	wrong	
	sign	knot	wrote	
		know		
		knowledge		
		knuckle		

TONGUE TWISTERS FROM A TO Z

In 1819, *Peter Piper's Practical Principles of Plain and Perfect Pronunciation* was published in England by J. Harris and Son. The book contained a tongue twister for each letter of the alphabet. Of these, "Peter Piper" still remains. Here are our new first lines for tongue twisters for each letter of the alphabet. In order to complete them, follow this pattern for "Peter Piper."

The first line is a statement.	Peter Piper picked a peck of pickled peppers.
The second line asks if the statement is true.	Did Peter Piper pick a peck of pickled peppers?
The third and fourth lines ask an "if" and "where" question.	If Peter Piper picked a peck of pickled peppers, where's the peck of pickled peppers Peter Piper picked?

Angela Abigail Applewhite ate anchovies and artichokes.

Bertha Bartholomew blew blue bubbles.

Clifford Cleaver clumsily closed the closet clasp.

Dwayne Dwiddle drew a drawing of dreaded Dracula.

Elmer Elwood eluded eleven elderly elephants.

Floyd Flingle flipped flat flapjacks.

Greta Gruber grabbed a group of green grapes.

Hattie Henderson hated happy hippos.

Ida Ivy identified the ivory iris.

Julie Jackson juggled the juicy, jiggly jello.

Karl Kessler kept the ketchup in the kitchen.

Lela Ladder lugged a lot of little lemons.

Milton Mallard mailed a mangled mango.

Newton Norton never needed new noodles.

Oscar Oliver ought to auction odd objects.

Patsy Planter plucked plump, purple, plastic plums.

Quincy Quist quite quickly quelled the quarreling quartet.

From *The Teacher's Book of Lists* ©1979, Goodyear Publishing Company, Inc.

Randy Rathbone wrapped a rather rare red rabbit.

Shelly Sherman shivered in a sheer, short shirt.

Trina Tweety tripped two twittering twins under a twiggy tree.

Uri Udall usually used his unicycle.

Vicky Vine viewed a very valuable vase.

Walter Worple warily warned the weary warrior.

Xerxes Xenon expected to xerox extra x-rays.

Yolanda Yarger yodeled yonder yesterday.

Ziggy Zine zig-zagged through the zoo zone.

Tongue-Twisting Activities

1. Make up twisters about people you know.
2. Make up twisters about products you use.
3. Make up a second line for a twister that does *not* follow the Peter Piper pattern.

   Hattie Henderson hated happy hippos.
   She hoped the hippos had a horrible holiday.
4. Illustrate the twisters.
5. Extend the twisters by adding adjectives and adverbs to them.

   Angela Abigail Applewhite *artfully* ate *angular* anchovies and *awesome* artichokes.
6. Complete each tongue twister in the form of "Peter Piper."

WORD TWINS, TRIPLETS, AND QUADRUPLETS

Twins

aches and pains
Aunt and Uncle
back and forth
black and blue
black and white
blood and guts
bread and butter
bright and shiny
bright-eyed and bushy-tailed
cake and ice cream
cat and mouse
cease and desist
chips and dip
cloak and dagger
coat and tie
cold and clammy
cops and robbers
cowboys and Indians
cup and saucer
cut and dried
cut and paste
dogs and cats
do's and don'ts
ebb and flow
fish and chips
foot-loose and fancy-free
hearts and flowers
hide and seek
high and dry
high and mighty
hill and dale
hither and yon
huff and puff
hugs and kisses
in and out
jump and shout

knife and fork
lathe and plaster
life and death
light and fluffy
long and short
lost and found
loud and clear
Mom and Dad
Mother and Father
nickel and dime
night and day
now or never
nuts and bolts
old and gray
on and off
open and closed
open and shut
paper and pencil
peace and quiet
pins and needles
potatoes and gravy
p's and q's
read and write
rest and relaxation
rise and fall
rise and shine
rough and ready
safe and sound
salt and pepper
shoes and socks
short but sweet
show and tell
slip and slide
sister and brother
soap and water
sound and fury
soup to nuts

spic and span
sticks and stones
stop and go
strange but true
strong and silent
sugar and spice
table and chairs
tortoise and the hare
toss and turn
up and down
vinegar and oil
wash and dry
whether or not
wild and wooly

Triplets

animal, vegetable or mineral
bacon, lettuce and tomato
bell, book and candle
coffee, tea or milk
hop, skip and a jump
men, women and children
reading, writing and arithmetic
red, white and blue
snap, crackle and pop
tall, dark and handsome
up, up and away

Quadruplets

ear, eyes, nose and throat
eeny, meeny, miney, moe
rain, hail, sleet or snow
rich man, poor man,
     beggarman, thief

From *The Teacher's Book of Lists* © 1979, Goodyear Publishing Company, Inc.

Activities With Word Twins, Triplets, and Quadruplets

1. List word pairs that can be reversed, such as night and day, cats and dogs, and sister and brother.

2. Group word pairs into categories such as foods, people, directions, and actions.

3. Use word pairs in sentences.

4. List word pairs that are opposites, such as long and short or rise and fall.

5. Find word pairs that repeat the same word, such as over and over, coast to coast, and higher and higher.

6. Find people that are often thought of in twosomes or threesomes, such as Laurel and Hardy, Sonny and Cher, and Larry, Moe, and Curly Joe.

Name _____

WORD TWINS CROSSWORD

Work the crossword puzzle by filling in the word that completes each twin or triplet.

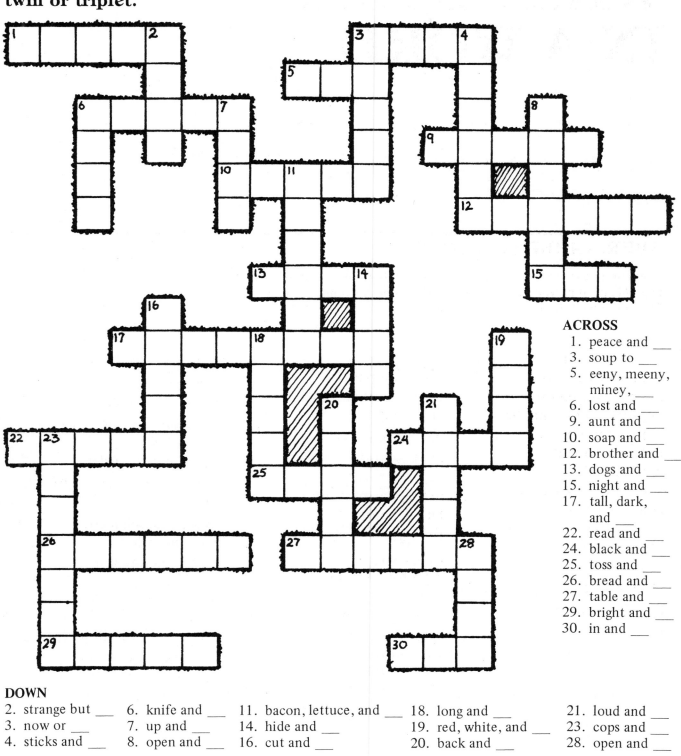

ACROSS
1. peace and ___
3. soup to ___
5. eeny, meeny, miney, ___
6. lost and ___
9. aunt and ___
10. soap and ___
12. brother and ___
13. dogs and ___
15. night and ___
17. tall, dark, and ___
22. read and ___
24. black and ___
25. toss and ___
26. bread and ___
27. table and ___
29. bright and ___
30. in and ___

DOWN
2. strange but ___
3. now or ___
4. sticks and ___
6. knife and ___
7. up and ___
8. open and ___
11. bacon, lettuce, and ___
14. hide and ___
16. cut and ___
18. long and ___
19. red, white, and ___
20. back and ___
21. loud and ___
23. cops and ___
28. open and ___

From *The Teacher's Book of Lists* ©1979, Goodyear Publishing Company, Inc.

two
WHAT'S NOT IN A WORD

ABBR. — ABBREVIATIONS

These often-used abbreviations are listed with their most common meanings. Many abbreviations have more than one meaning, such as *cont.* for continued, contents, and continent.

acct.—account
a.m.—before noon
anon.—anonymous
approx.—approximate
appt.—appointment
apt.—apartment
arr.—arrival
assn., assoc.—association
asst.—assistant
attn.—attention
atty.—attorney
Ave.—Avenue
avg.—average

beg.—beginning
bet.—between
bldg.—building
Blvd.—Boulevard

cc—carbon copy
chs.—chapters

clsd.—closed
Co.—Company
Corp.—Corporation
ctr.—center

dbl.—double
dent.—dentist
dep.—departure
dept.—department
Dr.—Doctor

E.—East
ea.—each
e.g.—for example
elem.—elementary
encl.—enclosure
ency.—encyclopedia
env.—envelope
est.—established
etc.—and so forth (etcetera)

Frwy.—Freeway

govt.—government
hosp.—hospital
Hwy.—Highway
ibid.—in the same place
    (ibidem)
id.—the same (idem)
illus.—illustration, illustrated
init.—initial
misc.—miscellaneous
mo.—month
mfg.—manufacturing
mgr.—manager
Mr.—form of address for a
    man
Mrs.—form of address for a
    married woman
Ms.—form of address for a
    woman

42

Mt., mts.—Mount, mountains

no.—number
N., No.—North
nos.—numbers
obs.—obsolete
p.—page
pd.—paid
perm.—permanent
pkg.—package
Pkwy.—Parkway
p.m.—after noon
pp.—pages
pr.—pair

recd.—received
Rd.—Road
rt.—right
Rte.—Route
S., So.—South
sta.—station
stmt.—statement
tel. no.—telephone number
v., vs.—versus
vocab.—vocabulary

W.—West
wk., wks.—week, weeks
w/—with
w/o—without
yrs.—yours

a.k.a.—also known as
a.s.a.p.—as soon as possible
b.l.t.—bacon, lettuce, tomato (sandwich)
c/o—care of
c.o.d.—cash on delivery
i.d.—identification
I.O.U.—I owe you
I.Q.—intelligence quotient
k.o.—knock out
m.p.g.—miles per gallon
m.p.h.—miles per hour

o.j.—orange juice
P.S.—written after (post scriptum)
r.p.m.—revolutions per minute
r.s.v.p.—please reply (respondez s'il vous plaît)
t.v.—television
v.i.p.—very important person

Days of the Week

Sun., Sund.—Sunday
Mon.—Monday
Tues., Tu.—Tuesday
Wed.—Wednesday
Thurs., Thur., Th.—Thursday
Fri., Fr.—Friday
Sat.—Saturday

Months of the Year

Jan.—January
Feb.—February
Mar.—March
Apr.—April
Jul.—July
Aug.—August
Sept.—September
Oct.—October
Nov.—November
Dec.—December

Parts of Speech

adj.—adjective
adv.—adverb
conj.—conjunction
n.—noun
prep.—preposition
v.—verb

Name _____

TELL-A-PHONE ANSWERING SERVICE

Rewrite the telephone messages, using complete words in place of each abbreviation.

MESSAGE

To: Sam
Call your apt.
mgr. a.s.a.p. about
the pkg. he
recd.

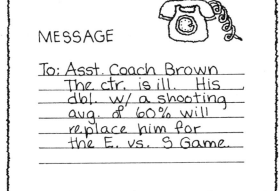

MESSAGE

To: Asst. Coach Brown
The ctr. is ill. His
dbl. w/ a shooting
avg. of 60% will
replace him for
the E. vs. S Game.

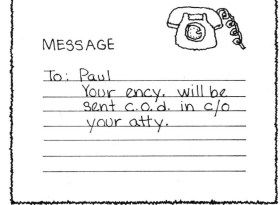

MESSAGE

To: Paul
Your ency. will be
sent c.o.d. in c/o
your atty.

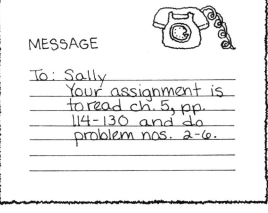

MESSAGE

To: Sally
Your assignment is
to read ch. 5, pp.
114-130 and do
problem nos. 2-6.

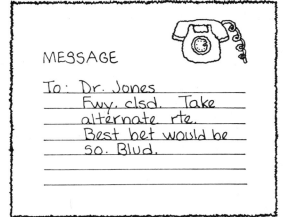

MESSAGE

To: Dr. Jones
Fwy. clsd. Take
alternate rte.
Best bet would be
So. Blvd.

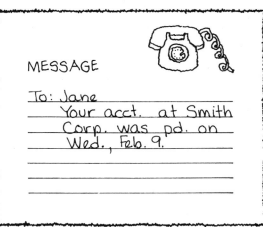

MESSAGE

To: Jane
Your acct. at Smith
Corp. was pd. on
Wed., Feb. 9.

From *The Teacher's Book of Lists* © 1979, Goodyear Publishing Company, Inc.

SHORT FORMS

Here are some short forms often used as words.

awol—absent without leave

bems—bug-eyed monsters (sci-fi jargon)

biz—business

caps—capital letters

celebs—celebrities

chimp—chimpanzee

co-op—a cooperative

copter—helicopter

croc—crocodile

cuke—cucumber

deejay—disc jockey

deli—delicatessen

emcee—master or mistress of ceremonies

exam—examination

flu—influenza

gator—alligator

gym—gymnasium

hi fi—high fidelity

hippo—hippopotamus

home ec—home economics

hood—hoodlum

hose—hosiery

info—information

lab—laboratory

limo—limousine

lube—lubricate, lubrication

math—mathematics

mayo—mayonnaise

memo—memorandum

morn—morning

mums—chrysanthemums

peke—pekinese dog

photo—photograph

pix—pictures

pj's—pajamas

P.O.—Post Office

reps—representatives

rhino—rhinoceros

sarge—sergeant

sax—saxophone

sci fi—science fiction

sitcom—situation comedy

thru—through

tux—tuxedo

ump—umpire

vet—veteran, veterinarian

wiz—wizard

Activities With Short Forms

1. Write advertising slogans containing short forms for products or jobs.

    Hire a *limo* from Mr. Nimo.   End each of your days
    in Smith's *P.J.'s.*

    For the answers to a quiz,
    go to see your local *wiz*.

2. Write sentences that contain several short forms.

    The *croc* and the *chimp* had *cukes* from the *deli*.

From *The Teacher's Book of Lists* © 1979, Goodyear Publishing Company, Inc.

3. Fill in phrase patterns with a short-form word and a word that rhymes with it.

_____ of _____

a _____ _____

the _____ by a _____

Examples of completed phrase patterns:

_____*rows*_____ of _____*hose*_____

a _____*large*_____ _____*sarge*_____

the _____*ump*_____ by a _____*dump*_____

the _____*chimp*_____ in a _____*blimp*_____

a _____*cuke*_____ for a _____*Duke*_____

a _____*cab*_____ with a _____*lab*_____

The completed phrases can be used:

a. as story titles;
b. as lines of poetry;
c. to make up silly questions;
d. to make silly stories by linking several phrases together.

CONTRACTIONS

aren't—are not
can't—cannot
couldn't—could not
didn't—did not
doesn't—does not
don't—do not
hadn't—had not
hasn't—has not
haven't—have not
isn't—is not
mightn't—might not
mustn't—must not
oughtn't—ought not
shouldn't—should not
wasn't—was not
weren't—were not
won't—will not
wouldn't—would not

I've—I have
they've—they have
you've—you have
we've—we have
he'd—he had, he would
I'd—I had, I would
she'd—she had, she would
they'd—they had, they would
we'd—we had, we would
you'd—you had, you would
we're—we are
you're—you are
there're—there are
they're—they are
I'm—I am
he's—he is, he has
it's—it is, it has

let's—let us
she's—she is, she has
that's—that is, that has
what's—what is, what has
where's—where is, where has
who's—who is, who has
I'll—I will, I shall
he'll—he will, he shall
it'll—it will, it shall
she'll—she will, she shall
they'll—they will, they shall
we'll—we will, we shall
who'll—who will, who shall
you'll—you will, you shall

PORTMANTEAUS

A portmanteau is a word formed by the arbitrary combination of two words. Lewis Carroll invented the portmanteaus *snark*, from snake and shark, and *slithy*, from slimy and lithe. Children can create their own portmanteaus from words on the Twins and Triplets List, page 39, or from familiar word pairs such as blue jeans, cottage cheese, and jump rope.

beefalo = beef + buffalo
bishaw = bicycle + rickshaw
botel = boat + hotel
broasted = broiled + roasted
brunch = breakfast + lunch

chortle = chuckle + snort

dumbfound = dumb + confound

eggler = egg + dealer
Eurasia = Europe + Asia

fantabulous = fantastic + fabulous
fishwich = fish + sandwich

galumphing = gallop + triumphing
guesstimate = guess + estimate

meld = melt + weld
mingy = mean + stingy
motel = motor + hotel
motorcade = motor car + cavalcade

smog = smoke + fog
splatter = splash + spatter
splotch = spot + blotch
splurge = splash + surge

vegeburger = vegetable + hamburger

From *The Teacher's Book of Lists* © 1979, Goodyear Publishing Company, Inc.

three
SPELLING

SPELLING ODDS AND ENDS

These ten words appear in more than a quarter of all that we write:

the   a
and   in
of   that
to   you
I   for

Some words from a grade-school spelling book published in 1845:

cornucopiae   amanuensis
bacchanalian   circumambient
pusillanimity

A 1950 article by Leslie W. Johnson cited these 5 words, from a list of 100, as most frequently misspelled by 14,643 children in the elementary grades.

their   they
too   then
there

These 5 were the least often misspelled of the 100:

jumped
around
dropped
babies
money

The longest word in Webster's New Collegiate Dictionary, 8th edition:

pneumonoultramicroscopicsilicovolcanoconiosis

The longest word in the Oxford English Dictionary:

floccinaucinihilipilification

The first spelling book was printed in 1643 by Stephen Day in Cambridge, Massachusetts.

100 SPELLING DEMONS

ache	color	grammar	many	shoes	Tuesday
again	coming	guess	meant	since	two
always	cough	half	minute	some	used
among	could	having	much	straight	very
answer	country	hear	none	sugar	wear
any	dear	heard	often	sure	Wednesday
been	doctor	here	once	tear	week
beginning	does	hoarse	piece	their	where
believe	done	hour	quiet	there	whether
blue	don't	instead	raise	they	which
break	early	just	read	though	whole
built	easy	knew	ready	through	women
business	enough	laid	said	tired	won't
busy	every	loose	says	tonight	would
buy	February	lose	seems	too	write
can't	forty	making	separate	trouble	writing
choose	friend			truly	wrote

From W.F. Jones, *A Concrete Investigation of the Materials of English Spelling,* University Press: University of South Dakota, 1913.

243 ADDITIONAL SPELLING DEMONS

abrupt	analyze	bicycle	committee	dining
absence	angle	breathe	conscience	disappear
accommodate	apologize	brilliant	continuous	disappoint
accumulate	apparently	bulletin	correspondence	discipline
accurate	appearance	calendar	courteous	disease
acquire	appreciate	campaign	criticism	dissatisfied
across	arctic	canceled	curiosity	division
address	argument	career	cylinder	eighth
adequate	arrangement	cemetery	decision	embarrass
adjourn	athletic	certain	definitely	environment
advice	audience	chief	difference	equipped
amateur	before	colonel	different	especially
analysis	benefited	column	difficulty	etc.

From *The Teacher's Book of Lists* ©1979, Goodyear Publishing Company, Inc.

exaggerate
excellent
existence
experience
extremely
familiar
fascinate
finally
foreign
formally
formerly
fulfill
fundamental
glimpse
gorgeous
government
governor
groceries
guarantee
guard
guidance
handsome
height
heroes
hoping
humorous
hurriedly
illegible
illustrate
imaginary
immediately
incidentally
independence
indispensable
intelligence
interesting
interpreted
interrupt
irrelevant
its
it's

jealous
jewelry
journey
judgment
khaki
kindergarten
knead
knowledge
laboratory
leisure
library
license
licorice
lightning
likely
listen
livelihood
loneliness
maintenance
maneuver
manufacture
marriage
mathematics
medicine
mileage
miniature
miscellaneous
mischievous
misspell
mortgage
muscle
naturally
necessary
nickel
niece
ninety
ninth
noticeable
nuisance

occasion
occur
occurred
o'clock
omission
omitted
opinion
opportunity
opposite
original
pamphlet
parallel
particular
pastime
peaceable
performance
permanent
personal
personnel
persuade
pleasant
possession
precede
privilege
probably
procedure
proceed
professor
pronunciation
psychology
pumpkin
pursue
quantity
quarrel
quite
realize
receive
recognize
recommend
rehearse
relevant
relief

relieve
religious
repetition
restaurant
rheumatism
rhubarb
rhythm
ridiculous
safety
schedule
scissors
seize
sergeant
severely
similar
sizable
souvenir
strength
studying
succeed
sufficient
surprise
temperature
temporary
tendency
therefore
thorough
together
tomorrow
tongue
transferred
typical
unanimous
undoubtedly
unique
unnecessary
until
usually
utensil

vacancy
vacuum
vegetable
vinegar
visible
volume
weather
wholly
who's
whose
yacht
yield
yolk
your
you're
youth
zealous

From *The Teacher's Book of Lists* © 1979, Goodyear Publishing Company, Inc.

A SPELLING LIST FOR TEACHERS

accept
achievement
address
adequate
adjust
administrator
adolescents
affect
aggressive
algebra
alternative
anonymous
anxiety
applies
argument
arithmetic
assignment
assistant
attitude
audio-visual
behavior
bookkeeping
boundaries
building
business
cafeteria
calendar
Catholic
census
certain
channels
children
choir
climbing
commercial
community
comparative
complaints
compulsory

conference
coordinator
correspondence
corridor
counselor
courteous
criticism
curriculum
decision
deficient
delinquency
democratic
despite
destructive
detention
different
diploma
disastrous
discipline.
discrimination
discussion
distraction
distribute
district
diverts
effect
elementary
entrance
epileptic
everything
excellent
exception
exercise
experiment
extension
faculty
field
foreign

genius
grammar
government
group
guidance
guilty
gymnasium
handicapped
hectic
height
heterogeneous
history
homogeneous
honorary
illiterate
immature
incidentally
independently
innocent
instructor
insurance
integration
intelligence
irate
irritated
janitor
journal
judgment
laid
languages
leisure
library
license
lounge
luncheon
Lutheran

mathematics
mischievous
motivated
municipal
necessary
negative
Negroes
observant
opportunities
orchestra
parental
parochial
perform
physics
pieces
plumbing
practically
practice
preference
prejudice
premises
preparatory
principal
professor
projector
psychiatric
quiet
quit
quite
receive
recess
recognize
reference
repetition
reprimand
requirements
responsible

salary
secondary
secretary
segregation
sensitive
significant
sincerely
smoking
sophomore
status
strength
student
suburban
successful
superintendent
supervisor
technology
tenure
theories
tried
truly
typical
ultimately
usually
vacancy
violent
vocational
(plus names of
local businesses,
streets, etc.)

Reprinted with permission from "When Teachers Misspell," *Improving College and University Teaching* (Spring, 1965).
Corvallis, Ore.: Oregon State University Press.

From *The Teacher's Book of Lists* © 1979, Goodyear Publishing Company, Inc.

FOR SYLLABIC SHOWOFFS

Most children love to impress family and friends by spelling long words or words with repetitive spelling patterns. Here's a list to show off with.

3 syllables	4 syllables	5 syllables	6 syllables
Chihuahua	Chattanooga	abracadabra	encyclopedia
committee	eucalyptus	auditorium	octogenarian
cucumber	gargantuan	bibliography	onomatopoeia
cumulus	gobbledegook	dieffenbachia	paleontology
discotheque	graduation	hippopotamus	
Frankenstein	harum-scarum	tonsillectomy	
labyrinth	hocus-pocus	whatchamacallit	
millionaire	independent	thingamadoodle	
	kookaburra		
	Minnehaha		
	Mississippi		
	Tallahassee		
	Transylvania		

12 syllables: antidisestablishmentarianism

14 syllables: supercalifragilisticexpialidocious

SPELLING PLURALS

Add *es* to words that end in *o* to make plurals.

buffalo*	motto*	embargo	torpedo
cargo*	potato	hero*	veto
domino*	tomato	mango*	volcano*
echo	tornado*		zero*

*These words add either *s* or *es*.

Add *es* to words that end in *s, ch, z, x*, or *sh* to make plurals.

ax	speech
buzz	splash
crush	tax
glass	topaz
guess	waltz
mash	watch
sandwich	wish

Change the *f* or *fe* to *v* before adding *es* to words that end in *f* or *fe* to make plur~~al~~

calf	~~c~~hief
half	~~w~~harf
knife	~~l~~ife
leaf	~~w~~olf

STOPPED AT SELF

Change the *y* to *i* before adding *es* to words that end in a consonant and *y* to make plurals.

ally	city	history	sky
apply	copy	lady	spy
army	cry	lily	story
baby	fairy	marry	worry
berry	fancy	mystery	
body	fly	reply	

IRREGULAR PLURALS

Singular	**Plural**
analysis	analyses
antenna	antennae
axis	axes
bacterium	bacteria
basis	bases
cactus	cactuses, cacti
child	children
crisis	crises
curriculum	curricula, curriculums
datum	data
die	dice
foot	feet
goose	geese
hippopotamus	hippopotamuses, hippopotami
man	men
medium	media
mouse	mice
nebula	nebulae
oasis	oases
ox	oxen
parenthesis	parentheses
phenomenon	phenomena
radius	radii
stratum	strata
tooth	teeth
woman	women

THE LAST WORD—NATIONAL SPELLING BEE WORDS

Here are the last words that have been spelled correctly by the winners
of the National Spelling Bee since 1970.

croissant	1970
shalloon	1971
macerate	1972
vouchsafe	1973
hydrophyte	1974
incisor	1975
narcolepsy	1976
cambist	1977

Here are 18 other words on which the championships have been won or
lost since the Spelling Bee began in 1926.

abbacy	esquamulose	propitiatory
acquiesced	eudaemonic	propylaeum
asceticism	gladiolus ·	psychiatry
brethren	larghetto	sacrilegious
cinnabar	onerous	transept
condominium	pronunciation	uncinated

four
PUT IT IN WRITING

WORDS USED INSTEAD OF "SAID"

More Common

added	crowed	nudged	stammered
admitted	dared	offered	stated
answered	decided	ordered	stuttered
argued	declared	panted	suggested
asked	demanded	pleaded	tempted
babbled	denied	praised	wailed
bawled	ended	prayed	wept
bet	exclaimed	promised	whispered
blurted	explained	questioned	wondered
bragged	fretted	quoted	yelled
bugged	gasped	ranted	
called	greeted	reminded	
cautioned	hinted	replied	
chatted	informed	requested	
cheered	insisted	roared	
chuckled	laughed	sassed	
coaxed	lied	sighed	
confessed	murmured	smiled	
corrected	muttered	smirked	
cried	named	snickered	
croaked	nodded		

Less Common

admonished	claimed	evinced	proffered	simpered
assented	conceded	indicated	projected	speculated
atoned	demurred	jeered	quibbled	sputtered
bantered	denounced	jested	quipped	squelched
bemoaned	disclosed	lamented	quizzed	stipulated
berated	drawled	leered	rebuked	stormed
broached	droned	mocked	rejoiced	theorized
cajoled	enjoined	needled	renounced	vocalized
carped	enumerated	opined	retorted	volunteered
challenged	espoused	outlined	revealed	
cited	estimated	presented	scowled	

Activities With "Said" Words

1.   To comic strip bubbles, add:

    1)   the name of the person speaking

    2)   a word from the *said* list to show how the person is speaking

    3)   any needed punctuation

2.   Make a matching game of statements and words for *said*.

3.   Categorize words with similar meanings into groups titled *pleading, anger, laughing, crying, asking,* and *answering*.

4.   Write a song title or lyric. Add a phrase to show how it might be said. For example: *"Tie a yellow ribbon 'round the old elm tree,"* reminded Tony.

5.   Add adverbs or phrases to words used instead of said to elaborate on how something is being spoken:

whispered softly   breathlessly gasped

whispered a little too loudly   gasped in a terrified way

Name

CARTOON CAPTIONS

Write a caption for each picture. For each caption choose a statement from column A and a word from column B that tells how the statement is being said. Be sure to punctuate the captions you write.

"Give me some water," gasped the flower.	*the chair.*
the menu.	*the soda pop.*
the calculator.	*the onion.*
the dictionary.	*the hamburger.*
the telephone.	*the refrigerator.*

A	B
Don't forget to close the door	cried
I guess I'll have a straw	decided
Won't you have a seat	corrected
Have a bite	called
Don't cut me with that knife	tempted
Your spelling is wrong	ordered
I'll have a steak, potato, and a salad	reminded
Answer me when I ring	invited
Also, two plus two makes four	added

From *The Teacher's Book of Lists* © 1979, Goodyear Publishing Company, Inc.

WORDS FOR RUN/WALK, LAUGH/CRY, SAD/HAPPY

Here are some alternatives for six words overused by children in their stories. Children can look them up and discuss the subtle differences between the words, and use them in the writing or editing of their stories.

Run	Walk	Laugh	Cry	Sad	Happy
bolt	amble	cackle	bawl	cheerless	blissful
chase	ambulate	chortle	blubber	crestfallen	blithe
dart	lumber	chuckle	howl	dejected	cheerful
dash	meander	crow	moan	depressed	delighted
flee	pace	giggle	sniffle	despondent	ecstatic
gallop	plod	grin	snivel	disheartened	elated
hurry	prance	guffaw	sob	dismal	exultant
jog	ramble	hoot	wail	dispirited	gay
lope	saunter	howl	weep	downcast	glad
race	shuffle	roar	whimper	downhearted	gleeful
rush	stagger	smile	whine	forlorn	jolly
scamper	step	snicker		joyless	jovial
scoot	stride	titter		melancholy	joyful
scramble	stroll			miserable	jubilant
scurry	strut			mournful	lighthearted
scuttle	swagger			pitiable	mirthful
speed	totter			sorrowful	overjoyed
sprint	trek			sorry	sunny
tear	trudge			unhappy	thrilled
trot				woebegone	tickled
				woeful	
				wretched	

From *The Teacher's Book of Lists* © 1979, Goodyear Publishing Company, Inc.

SIMILES

Here are some similes that are as old as the hills, and activities to stimulate the writing of new ones.

as big as a house

as black as coal

as blind as a bat

as brown as a berry

as busy as a bee

as clean as a whistle

as clear as crystal

as cool as a cucumber

as easy as pie

as flat as a pancake

as fresh as a daisy

as good as gold

as happy as a lark

as hard as a rock

as light as a feather

as limp as a wet noodle

as mad as a hornet

as meek as a lamb

as neat as a pin

as pale as a ghost

as playful as a kitten

as pretty as a picture

as quick as a wink

as quiet as a mouse

as red as a beet

as sharp as a tack

as sick as a dog

as slippery as an eel

as slow as molasses

as sly as a fox

as smooth as silk

as stiff as a board

as straight as an arrow

as stubborn as a mule

as warm as toast

as white as a sheet

as wise as an owl

Activities With Similes

1. Make up new similes for the same descriptive adjectives as some of the examples on the list. *Example:* as big as a mountain

2. Make up similes that are completed by phrases.
    as slippery as a newly polished dance floor
    as easy as turning on the tap

3. Make up some comical similes to communicate the opposite meaning of an adjective. *Examples:*
    "As clear as mud" means something was not clear at all.
    as heavy as a bag of marshmallows
    as pretty as Frankenstein's mother

4. Make up groups of similes.
    similes for color words: as purple as a royal robe
    similes that use animals as the basis of comparison: as jumpy as a kangaroo
    similes for feeling words: as sad as the kittens who lost their mittens
    similes that name famous people: as tall as Wilt Chamberlain
    similes that are alliterative: as slow as a sloth; as rigid as a robot

5. Make up similes using the word "like."
    A tree is like a chemical factory.
    The catsup oozed across the hamburger like lava trailing down the side of the volcano.

Name _____

From *The Teacher's Book of Lists* © 1979, Goodyear Publishing Company, Inc.

SIMILE FACTORY

Directions: Take the words through the Simile Factory. Complete each simile according to the directions on each machine.

From *The Teacher's Book of Lists* © 1979, Goodyear Publishing Company, Inc.

GOOD VS. EVIL WORDS

Superstition, magic, mystery, and spooky tales have great appeal for children of all ages. These Good vs. Evil Words can be used to stimulate discussion, research, and story writing.

abracadabra	elf	Mars	spilling salt
amulet	evil eye	mascot	spirits
banshee	fairy	moon	stars
bewitch	fear	mustard seed	step on a crack
black cat	find a penny	occult	stub your toe
Blarney Stone	fire	omen	sun
bride's garter	four-leaf clover	opal	taboo
broken mirror	Friday the 13th	Pan	toad
bubbles on coffee	fungi	poltergeist	totem
buckeye	genie	Puck	triangle
Ceres	Gesundheit	rabbit's foot	troll
charms	ghost	rainbow	two-dollar bill
copper bracelet,	gnome	rat tail	voodoo
anklet	goblin	rice	werewolf
cross	ground-hog day	rites	witch
cross your fingers	horseshoe	robin	zaps
cures	imp	ruby	Zeus
curse	knock on wood	seventh child	Zodiac
demon	walk under ladder	signs	#7
devil	Leo	snake	#13
Druid	luck	sneezing	#3
Dryad	lycanthropy	Sol	
dwarf	Magi	soul	

FLIP-FLOP WORDS

abba-dabba	click-clack	ducky-wucky	giggle-gaggle	hoity-toity
bibble-babble	clickety-clackety	even-Steven	hanky-panky	hokey-pokey
boo-hoo	clip-clop	fiddle-faddle	harum-scarum	hootchie-cootchie
boogie-woogie	dilly-dally	flim-flam	heebie-jeebies	hully-gully
bow-wow	ding-a-ling	flip-flop	helter-skelter	humpty-dumpty
chiller-diller	ding-dong	fuddy-duddy	hippety-hoppety	hurdy-gurdy
chit-chat	dribble-drabble	fuzzy-wuzzy	hocus-pocus	hurly-burly

From The Teacher's Book of Lists © 1979, Goodyear Publishing Company, Inc.

itsy-bitsy	piggly-wiggly	rub-dub	ticky-tacky	wiggle-waggle
jibber-jabber	piggy-wiggy	scribble-scrabble	tip-top	willy-nilly
jingle-jangle	ping-pong	see-saw	tippety-toppety	wishy-washy
lovey-dovey	pitter-patter	shilly-shally	tootsie-wootsie	yakety-yak
mish-mash	plip-plop	splish-splash	trip-trap	zig-zag
mumbo-jumbo	raggle-taggle	super-duper	walkie-talkie	
namby-pamby	razzle-dazzle	teeny-weeny	whing-ding	
okey-dokey	rinky-dinky	teensy-weensy	wibble-wobble	
palsy-walsy	rowdy-dowdy	tick-tock	wig-wag	

Activities With Flip-Flop Words

1. Choose several flip-flop words. Write short stories in which the flip-flop words repeat themselves, or appear in a pattern, such as in Rikki-Tikki-Tembo or The Three Billy Goats Gruff.

2. Find flip-flop words that name sounds. Use the words to represent sounds in sentences.

    "Trip-trap, trip-trap" went the boots on the bridge.

    The "click-clack" of the crickets became softer at dawn.

3. Make up story titles that include a flip-flop word and another word that is related by sound or meaning.

    The Wishy-Washy Laundry

    The Jibber-Jabber Gypsies

    The Super-Duper Blooper

SECRET WRITING—CODES AND CIPHERS

Spacing Code

A super-simple position code is made by merely changing the position of the spaces between words.

> DANGEROUS TO REMAIN LEAVE AT ONCE
> DA NGERO USTOR EMAI NLEA VEATO NCE

Every Other Letter Cipher

This is a very simple cipher, in which random letters are inserted between each letter of the actual message, and then all the letters are grouped into "words" of five letters each. The cipher begins with a random letter. Meaningless letters may be added to the last "word" to complete the five-letter pattern. The message SECRET MEETING AT BLACK LAGOON would look something like this, depending on the random letters selected:

TSREF CLRNE QTXMS ELERT PIKNR GVAMT NBOLR ADCEK MLPAG GIOLO SNRTU

Double Parallel-Alphabet Cipher

Select a key word of at least seven letters that does not use the same letter twice. Following it, write the alphabet omitting any letter found within the key word. Now write the alphabet beneath this.

G E R M A N Y B C D F H I J K L O P Q S T U V W X Z
A B C D E F G H I J K L M N O P Q R S T U V W X Y Z

The message WATCH OUT, becomes VGSRB KTS using this cipher.

Alphabet Strips

Write the alphabet with an even space between each letter on a strip of paper. Now, on a longer strip, write the alphabet twice, again with an even space between each letter. A letter is agreed upon as the code name. Place the shorter strip above this letter on the longer strip. Then write the message in letters from the lower strip. Here is the set-up for a "D" code.

A B C D E F G H I J K L M N O P Q R S T U V W X Y Z

A B C D E F G H I J K L M N O P Q R S T U V W X Y Z A B C D E F

Here is a "D" code message: SODB LW VDIH

Chinese Cipher

The Chinese Cipher is a simple transposition cipher in which the letters of the message are written up and down columns, beginning in the upper right-hand corner.* MEET ME AT THE SHIP AT MIDNIGHT would first be written in columns like this:

N D E H M
I I S T E
G M H T E
H T I A T
T A P E M

The coded message would then be written: NDEHM IISTE GMHTE HTIAT TAPEM

*Meaningless letters may be added to the columns to complete the pattern.

From *The Teacher's Book of Lists* © 1979, Goodyear Publishing Company, Inc.

Bacon's Cipher

Francis Bacon, the English philosopher and author, invented this cipher which uses only two letters of the alphabet (a and b) in various combinations.

A	aaaaa	N	abbaa
B	aaaab	O	abbab
C	aaaba	P	abbba
D	aaabb	Q	abbbb
E	aabaa	R	baaaa
F	aabab	S	baaab
G	aabba	T	baaba
H	aabbb	UV	baabb
IJ	abaaa	W	babaa
K	abaab	X	babab
L	ababa	Y	babba
M	ababb	Z	babbb

Using this cipher, URGENT would read:

baabbbaaaaaabbaaabaaabbaabaaba

Tic Tac Toe Cipher

The letters of the alphabet are first arranged in a diagram.

AB	CD	EF
GH	IJ	KL
MN	OP	QR

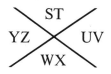

For the first letter of any pair, draw that part of the diagram. For the second letter of any pair, draw that part of the diagram, and add a dot. For example,

I = ☐   J = ☐•   U = <   T = ⌄

The message SEND MONEY IMMEDIATELY would be written:

DECODEABLE STATE MOTTOES

These state mottoes can be decoded using the codes on pages 62-64.

Spacing Code:

    LIB ERTYA NDUN IONN OWA NDFO REVE RONEA NDINS EPA RAB LE

Every Other Letter Cipher:

    FAPLO LSFTO XRUOY UPRMC DOPUG NHTAR LYSOT

Double Parallel Alphabet Cipher:

    SBA HGQS NPKJSCAP

Alphabet Strip in "D" code:

    OLEHUWB DQG SURVSHULWB

Chinese Cipher:

    EDYTV NNARI CENER EPDBT OEIIU SDNLE

Bacon's Cipher:

    aabaababababaaabaaabaaababababaaabaabaaaabbabbaaaaabbbabaaaabbaaabbbaabaabaaaa

Tic Tac Toe Cipher:

CODEABLE STATE MOTTOES AND NICKNAMES

Alabama	Audemus jura nostra defendere
	We dare to defend our rights
	Cotton state
Alaska	North to the future
	The last frontier
Arizona	Ditat Deus
	God enriches
	Grand Canyon state
Arkansas	Regnat populus
	The people rule; Land of opportunity
	Wonder state
California	Eureka
	I've found it
	Golden state

Colorado	Nil sine numine
	Nothing without the deity
	Centennial state
Connecticut	Qui transtulit sustinet
	He who transplanted continues to sustain
	Constitution state, Nutmeg state
Delaware	Liberty and Independence
	Diamond state, Blue Hen state, First state
Florida	In God we trust
	Peninsula state, Sunshine state
Georgia	Wisdom, justice, moderation
	Empire State of the South, Peach state
Hawaii	Ua mau ke ea o ka aina i ka pono
	The life of the land is perpetuated in righteousness
	Aloha state
Idaho	Esto perpetua
	Mayest thou endure forever
	Gem state
Illinois	State, sovereignty, national union
	Prairie state, Sucker state, Inland Empire
Indiana	The crossroads of America
	Hoosier state
Iowa	Our liberties we prize, and rights we maintain
	Hawkeye state
Kansas	Ad astra per aspera
	To the stars through difficulties
	Sunflower state, Jayhawker state
Kentucky	United we stand, divided we fall
	Blue grass state, Corncracker state
Louisiana	Union, justice, and confidence
	Pelican state, Creole state
Maine	Dirigo
	I guide
	Pine Tree state
Maryland	Scuto bonae voluntatis tuae coronasti nos
	With the shield of thy goodwill thou hast covered us
	Old-Line state, Free state
Massachusetts	Ense petit placidam sub libertate quietem
	By the sword we seek peace, but peace only under liberty
	Bay state, Old Colony state

Michigan	Si quaeris peninsulam amoenam circumspice
	If you seek a pleasant peninsula, look around you
	Wolverine state, Great Lake state
Minnesota	L'étoile du nord
	The star of the north
	Gopher state, North Star state
Mississippi	Virtute et armis
	By valor and arms
	Bayou state, Magnolia state
Missouri	Salus populi suprema lex esto
	Let the welfare of the people be the supreme law
	Show Me state
Montana	Oro y plata
	Gold and silver
	Treasure state
Nebraska	Equality before the law
	Cornhusker state, Tree Planter state
Nevada	All for our country
	Sagebrush state, Silver state
New Hampshire	Live free or die
	Granite state
New Jersey	Liberty and prosperity
	Garden state
New Mexico	Crescit eundo
	It grows as it goes
	Sunshine state, Land of Enchantment
New York	Excelsior
	Higher
	Empire state
North Carolina	Esse quam videri
	To be rather than to seem
	Tarheel state, Turpentine state
North Dakota	Liberty and union, now and forever, one and inseparable
	Sioux state, Flickertail state
Ohio	With God, all things are possible
	Buckeye state
Oklahoma	Labor omnia vincit
	Labor conquers all things
	Sooner state
Oregon	The union
	Beaver state

Pennsylvania	Virtue, liberty, and independence
	Keystone state
Rhode Island	Hope
	Little Rhody state
South Carolina	Animis opibusque parati
	Ready in soul and resource
	Palmetto state
South Dakota	Under God the people rule
	Coyote state
Tennessee	Agriculture and commerce
	Volunteer state
Texas	Friendship
	Lone Star state
Utah	Industry
	Beehive state
Vermont	Freedom and unity
	Green Mountain state
Virginia	Sic semper tyrannis
	Thus ever to tyrants
	Old Dominion state
Washington	Alki
	By and by
	Evergreen state
West Virginia	Montani semper liberi
	Mountaineers are always free men
	Mountain state
Wisconsin	Forward
	Badger state
Wyoming	Cedant arma togae
	Let arms yield to the gown
	Equality state

LETTER-WRITING ADDRESSES

Here's a list of addresses to give children so that they can write real letters to real places and people, and wait for real replies.

Baseball Commissioner's Office
75 Rockefeller Plaza
New York, New York 10019

National League Office (baseball)
Mills Building
220 Montgomery Street
San Francisco, California 94104

American League Office (baseball)
280 Park Avenue
New York, New York 10017

National Hockey League Headquarters
920 Sun Life Building
Montreal, Quebec H3B 2W2

National Basketball Association
League Office
2 Pennsylvania Plaza, Suite 2010
New York, New York 10001

National Football League Office
410 Park Avenue
New York, New York 10022

NASA
Lyndon B. Johnson Space Center
Houston, Texas 77058

World Wildlife Fund
Suite 728
910 – 17th Street N.W.
Washington, D.C. 20036

National Audubon Society
1130 5th Avenue
New York, New York 10028

International Frisbee Association
P.O. Box 4578
North Hollywood, California 91607

Circus Fans Association of America
P.O. Box 605
Aurora, Illinois 60507

National Dairy Council
6300 North River Road
Rosemont, Illinois 60018

National Hot Rod Association
10639 Riverside Drive
North Hollywood, California 91602

Society of American Magicians
66 Marked Tree Road
Needham, Massachusetts 02192

National Model Railroad Association
7061 Twin Oaks Drive
Indianapolis, Indiana 46226

American Numismatic Association
818 North Cascade
Colorado Springs, Colorado 80903

U.S. Table Tennis Association
Box 815
Orange, Connecticut 06477

National Investigations Committee
  on Unidentified Flying Objects
7970 Woodman Avenue
Van Nuys, California 91402

International Kitefliers Association
c/o Mr. Will Yolen
321 East 48th Street
New York, New York 10017

Bureau of Consumer Protection
Federal Trade Commission
Washington, D.C. 20580

From *The Teacher's Book of Lists* ©1979, Goodyear Publishing Company, Inc.

IUCN (International Union for the
    Conservation of Nature)
1110 Morges
Switzerland

Walt Disney Productions
500 South Buena Vista Street
Burbank, California 91521

NBC-TV
3000 West Alameda Avenue
Burbank, California 91505
      or
30 Rockefeller Plaza
New York, New York 10020

International Friendship League, Inc.
  (pen-pals)
40 Mount Vernon Street
Boston, Massachusetts 02108

Common Cause
2030 M Street, N.W.
Washington, D.C. 20036

CBS Television
7800 Beverly Boulevard
Los Angeles, California 90036

REBUS WORDS

Whenever block letters appear in the following words, the letter name is
pronounced; whereas sounds are to be pronounced for lower case
letters. For example, [rebus image] for tease and [rebus image] for belt.

are	belly	eerie	
ate		elbow	
be	belt		
beautiful	boat	fancy	
beauty		for	
bee	can		
bees	cartoon	glasses	
before			
belief	cookie		
	delight	handy	

From *The Teacher's Book of Lists* © 1979 Goodyear Publishing Company, Inc.

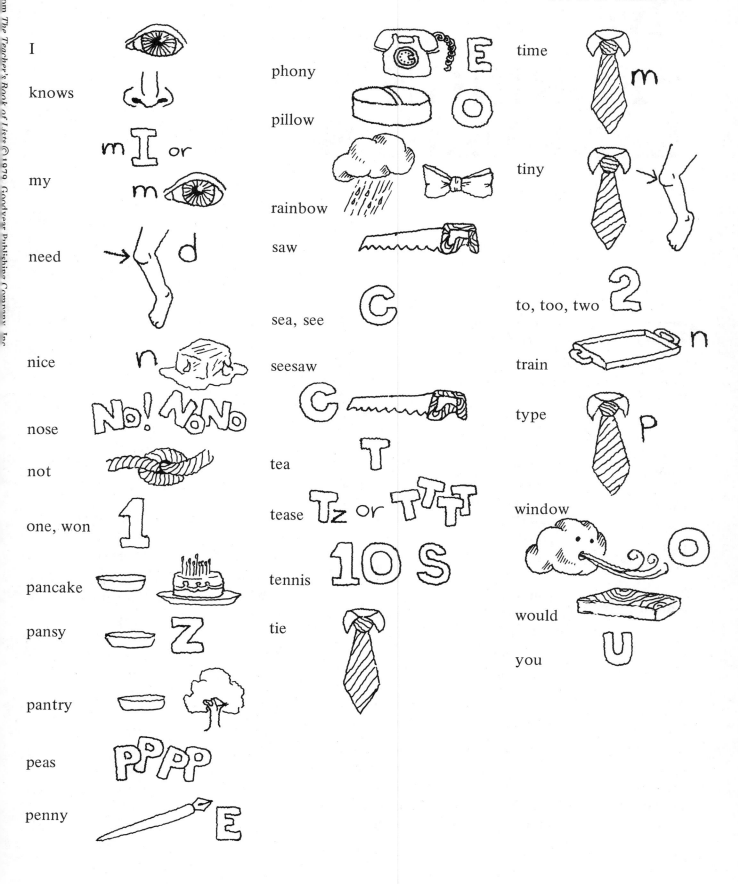

From *The Teacher's Book of Lists* ©1979, Goodyear Publishing Company, Inc.

five
"FOREIGN" LANGUAGES

BORROWED WORDS

We have adopted the following words from other languages with only some minor spelling changes. Sometimes the original spelling will appear for its interest value.

African

goober
gumbo
okra
tote
voodoo
yam
zombie

American Indian

canoe
caucus
chipmunk
hickory
  (pohickery)
hominy
mackinaw
moccasin
moose
opossum
papoose
pecan
persimmon
powwow
raccoon
skunk (segongw)
squash
squaw
succotash
  (msiquatash)
toboggan
tomahawk
totem
wampum
wigwam

Arabic

alcohol
algebra
azimuth
caliph
fakir
genie (jinnī)
harem
hashish
lemon (limun)
magazine
mattress
mufti
muslim
rubaiyat
sahib
sherbet
sofa
tariff
zero

Australian Aborigine

boomerang
kangaroo
kiwi
koala
wombat

Basque

jai alai

Chinese

chop suey
chow mein
gung ho
ketchup
kowtow
kumquat
tea

Dutch

brandy
Bronx
clipper
coleslaw
  (kool sla)
cruise
gin
Harlem
schooner
sloop
waffle (wafel)
Yonkers

East Indian (Hindi, Sanskrit)

bandana
bungalow
cashmere
cheetah
chintz
chutney
dinghy
dungarees
gunny
guru
jute
karma
loot
madras

polo
pundit
rajah
shampoo
swami
yoga

Egyptian

gum
pharaoh

Eskimo

caribou
kayak

French

amour
au gratin
avant-garde
beret
bistro
bonbon
bourbon
cadet
cadre
café
camaraderie
camouflage
carafe
cartel
champagne
chef
chiffon
cliché
clique
collage
commune
corsage
crêpe

crevasse
critique
crochet
croutons
decor
enclave
entrée
foyer
fuselage
garage
lecture
levee
litre
mademoiselle
masseur
montage
motif
naiveté
parfait
parole
partisan
pastel
penchant
portage
purée
rapport
reprise
revue
ricochet
rouge
roulette
sabotage
saboteur
sauté
savant
suite
timbre
toupee
vignette

German

blitzkrieg
cobalt
dachshund
delicatessen
dumb
edelweiss
fahrenheit
frau
fraulein
hamburger
herr
kaiser
kindergarten
leitmotiv
limburger
loafer
nickel
noodle
poodle
pretzel
pumpernickel
putsch
quartz
riesling
sauerkraut
schnapps
schnitzel
Volkswagen
waltz
wurst

Greek

asphasia
aura
circus
dialect
diaspora
dogma
eureka

genesis
nausea
paranoia
phobia
psyche
psychosis
schema

Haitian

barbecue
   (barbacoa)
cassava
manioc

Hebrew

amen
cinnamon
   (qinnamon)
hallelujah
jubilee
kibbutz
messiah
rabbi
shalom

Hungarian

coach
goulash
hussar
paprika

Italian

allegro
andante
balcony
balloon
bandit

baroque
bravo
broccoli
cacciatore
cadenza
cameo
cantata
fiasco
fresco
madonna
minestrone
oratorio
pasta
pianissimo
pilot
portico
prima donna
regatta
replica
salvo
sirocco
soprano
staccato
studio
trombone
vibrato
violin

Japanese

geisha
haiku
ju-jitsu
kabuki
kimono
nisei
rickshaw
samurai
soy
tempura
teriyaki
tycoon

From *The Teacher's Book of Lists* ©1979, Goodyear Publishing Company, Inc.

Latin

abacus
ad hoc
alias
alibi
alma mater
alumnus
auditor
axis
bacillus
calculus
campus
cancer
dictum
etcetera
extra
forum
fungus
gratis
humus
integer
juxta
per diem
per se
pro rata
quantum
quid pro quo
ratio
recipe
regalia
rostrum
solitaire
spatula
subpoena
symposium
tabula rasa
tibia
toga
trivia
ultra

Malay

amuck
bamboo
caddy
cockatoo
gingham
gong
mango
paddy
sarong

Persian

bazaar
caravan
divan
mogul
shah
shawl

Polish

polka

Polynesian

taboo
tattoo
ukulele

Portuguese

albino
fetish
marmalade
molasses

Russian

intelligentsia
kremlin
pogrom
samovar
steppe
tundra
vodka

Scandinavian

egg
fiord
ill
saga
ski
skin
skirt
smorgasbord

South American Indian

quinine
tapioca
tapir

Spanish

adobe
amigo
banana
bolero
bonanza
bronco
burro
caballero
canyon
chili
cocoa
corral
coyote
fiesta
gaucho
gringo
hombre
junta
lariat
machete
macho
mariachi
marimba
mesa
mesquite
mustang
padre
paella
palomino
patio
plaza
poncho
pueblo
rodeo
señor
sierra
simpatico
sombrero
stampede
tamale
tomato
tortilla
vigilante

Yiddish

bagel
blintzes
chutzpah
kibitzer
kosher
nosh
schlemiel
schlepp
schmaltz

Activities With Borrowed Words

1. Categorize words into groups, such as foods, people, clothing, animals, furniture, objects, places, verbs, and adjectives. Do you notice a certain pattern in the types of words we've borrowed from each language?

2. Draw a word origins world map.

3. Make up a story using as many borrowed words as you can.

   Herr Schmidt's *broccoli ricocheted* across the *fiord* and landed in *Mademoiselle's foyer* on top of her *moccasins.*

4. Use the library and dictionaries to trace the origin and development of several borrowed words.

5. Make up analogies using several of the borrowed words.

   Moccasin is to feet as *beret* is to head; *garage* is to *Volkswagen* as *corral* is to *bronco.*

6. Look up borrowed words in a dictionary that lists word etymologies and show the word's spelling and meaning in the original language.

   magazine = makhazin (Arabic)—a storehouse
   sherbet = sharbah (Arabic)—a cool drink
   ketchup = ke-tsiap (Chinese)—a brine from pickled fish, used as a sauce

BORROWED PHRASES

French

à la carte—meal dishes separately priced
au contraire—on the contrary
au courant—up to date
au naturel—in a natural state
au revoir—goodbye
bête noir—pet aversion
bon voyage—have a good journey
cause célèbre—situation arousing attention; noted incident
c'est la vie—that's life
cherchez la femme—a woman caused it: look for the woman

From *The Teacher's Book of Lists* © 1979, Goodyear Publishing Company, Inc.

coup de grâce—final, decisive action
coup d'état—a sudden change in government, often caused by force
creme de la crème—the very best
de rigeur—indispensable; required by fashion or custom
double entendre—double meaning
en masse—as a group
fait accompli—an accomplished and irrevocable fact or action
faux pas—a social error
hors d'ouevre—appetizer
joie de vivre—zest or enthusiasm for the pleasures of life
laissez faire—policy of noninterference
nom de plume—pen name
nouveau riche—newly or recently rich
par excellence—of highest quality
pièce de resistance—major or chief item of a series
raison d'être—reason for being
sans souci—without worry
savoir faire—sophistication; know-how
tour de force—feat of strength or brilliance
vis-à-vis—face to face; in relation to

German

auf Wiedersehen—till we meet again

Greek

hoi polloi—the general mass of people

Latin

ad hoc—for the present situation; temporary
ad infinitum—without limit
ad nauseam—to the point of disgust
alter ego—one's other self; a confidential friend
bona fide—sincere; genuine
caveat emptor—let the buyer beware
ex post facto—after the fact, retroactive
in extremis—near death
in toto—entirely
mea culpa—I'm guilty

modus operandi—method of operation
non sequitur—illogical; conclusion that does not follow from the evidence
persona non grata—an unwelcome or unacceptable person
rara avis—an unusual person or thing
status quo—the situation as is, without change
sub rosa—privately; secretly
tempus fugit—time flies
vox populi—the voice of the people

Spanish

Quien sabe?—Who knows?
Vaya con Dios—May God be with you

IGPAY ATINLAY AND OTHER SECRET LANGUAGES

Although examples have been given in writing, all of these secret
languages are meant to be spoken, not written.

Pig Latin

To speak Pig Latin, take the first letter or the consonant blend from the beginning of a
word, put it at the end of the word and add the sound *ay* to it. To all words beginning
with a vowel, leave the word as is and add *way* to the end of it.
Jack and Jill went up the hill becomes:
   ACKJAY ANDWAY ILLJAY ENTWAY UPWAY ETHAY ILLHAY

Na and Gree

To speak Na or Gree add *na* or *gree* to the end of each word.
   JACKNA ANDNA JILLNA WENTNA UPNA THENA HILLNA
or   JACKGREE ANDGREE JILLGREE WENTGREE UPGREE THEGREE HILLGREE

Skimono Jive

To speak Skimono Jive, add *sk* to the beginning of each word.
   SKJACK SKAND SKJILL SKWENT SKUP SKTHE SKHILL

Ong

To speak ong, add *ong* before every vowel sound.
   JONGACK ONGAND JONGILL WONGENT ONGUP THONGE HONGILL

Pelf Latin or Alfalfa

To speak Pelf or Alfalfa insert *lf* after every vowel sound and then repeat the vowel sound.
   JALFACK ALFAND JILFILL WELFENT ULFUP THELFE HILFILL

G or Goose Language

To speak G or Goose Language insert a *g* after the beginning sound in each syllable.
   JGACK AGND JGILL WGENT UGP THGE HGILL
This might sound something like this:
   Juhgack′agand′juhgill′wegent′uhgup′thuhguh′higill′

COCKNEY RHYMING SLANG

Rhyming slang became highly developed among the thieves of early- to mid-nineteenth-century London. Using it helped keep secrets from outsiders who might overhear a conversation. Although rhyming slang later spread to Australia, it is still generally known as Cockney Rhyming Slang.

alone—Pat Malone
arm—false alarm
bed—Uncle Ned
boots—daisy roots
bread—strike me dead
butter—roll me in the gutter
cake—give and take
cheese—balmy breeze, cough and sneeze, or stand at ease
coat—I'm afloat
corner—Johnny Horner
crook—babbling brook
cupboard—Mother Hubbard
dead—brown bread
dinner—Lilley and Skinner
dollar—Oxford scholar
ears—butter and beers
face—chevy chase
feet—plates o' meat
finger—lean and linger
flowers—happy half-hours
girl—twist and twirl

good—Robin Hood
hands—German bands
hat—lean and fat or tit for tat
head—loaf of bread or lump of lead
husband (old man)—pot and pan
I—mince pie
jail—jug and pail
knees—two's and three's
mate—china plate
Missus—cows and kisses
money—bees and honey or sugar and honey
mother—one another
mouth—north and south
neck—bushel and peck
night—flying kite
nose—I suppose
paper or newspaper—linen draper
pillow—weeping willow
pipe—cherry ripe
plate—Harry Tate
pocket—sky rocket
policeman (cop)—John Hop

room—shovel and broom
shirt—Dickey dirt
sick—Pat and Mick or Uncle Dick
sister—skin and blister
sleep or asleep—Bopeep
socks—almond rocks
stairs—apples and pears
steal (pinch)—half inch
street—fields of wheat
table—Cain and Abel

talk—bowl of chalk
tea—bug and flea or sweet pea
tobacco—nosey-me-knacker
trousers—round me houses or round the
    houses
umbrella—Isabella
walk—whisper and talk
water—fisherman's daughter
wife—trouble and strife

Mince pie put on my Dickey dirt and new daisy roots and went down the apples and pears to see the cows and kisses.

Activities With Rhyming Slang

1. Use the rhyming slang phrases in writing sentences and short stories.
2. Make up your own rhyming slang phrases.
3. Collect rhyming phrases such as hot shot, culture vulture, and sure cure.

SLANG WORDS AND PHRASES

We no longer need to consult a dictionary for the meanings of *hubbub, clumsy, bogus,* or *beat it,* used by Shakespeare, or for *bones* (dice) used by Chaucer. These words were considered slang in their times. Today's slang terms often have multiple meanings and are more difficult to define precisely. To provide a challenging activity, duplicate this list *without* definitions and ask the children to supply their own meanings.

all right—expression of emphatic agreement; exclamation of approval
bag—a special interest or enthusiasm
blew it—failed or missed an opportunity
blow your mind—to be overwhelmed or deeply impressed
bombed out (bombed)—failed or did very poorly
bummer—a bad experience or situation
cool—pleasing; in good taste
cool it—calm down
cop out—to renege on a plan or a promise

cracked up—had a fit of laughter
dig—to understand or enjoy; to notice or look at someone
downer—a depressing experience or situation
drag—boring; tedious person, thing, or event
dynamite—fantastic; terrific
far out—expression of approval; out of the ordinary
flake—unpredictable, irresponsible person
fox—attractive female
freak—person who likes a certain thing to an extreme
freak out—become irrational; shock others by unconventional behavior
funk, in a—in a depressed mood
funky—pleasing in an out-of-the-ordinary way
groovy—very good
hairy—frightening; difficult; exciting
hang in there—refuse to give in
hang tough—refuse to give in
heavy—deep; meaningful; profound
hung up—obsessed with; devoted to
hype—trick, deceive; promote
hyped up—overly excited
jive—tease; deceive
kicky—in fashion; exciting
laid back—easygoing; low-keyed
kinky—bizarre; peculiar
nerd, nurd—a person not in the know; a "square"
no sweat—no problem; easily
out of sight—great; wonderful
out of it—not involved with the present situation; not in the know; "square"
pad—place where a person lives
plastic—artificial
psyched out—fooled, misled; lost nerve or control due to fear or anxiety
psyched up—mentally prepared
put down—humiliating act or remark
really—a statement of agreement
right on—exclamation of approval
rip off—to steal; to defraud
solid—great; wonderful
spaced—not in touch with reality
tee'd off—angry
turkey—inferior, ineffective, incompetent person or thing
turn-on—interesting or exciting person or thing
unreal—unbelievably wonderful

up front—honest; open
uptight—anxious; rigid
wimp—a meek, uninteresting person
wiped out—tired; exhausted

Activities With Slang Words and Phrases

1.   Make "Slang Synonym Serpents."

2.   Define slang words and phrases using other slang in your definitions.

3.   Many of the slang words and phrases can be used to name or describe people, situations, or feelings. Categorize the words into these groups.

PEOPLE	SITUATIONS	FEELINGS
flake	bummer	in a funk
cool	cool	

4.   Expand the list of slang words and phrases by adding other forms of the terms. Indicate what part of speech they are and write sentences to show how they are used.

rip off (noun)   The rock concert was a real rip off.
rip off (verb)   Jeff was ripped off at the used car lot.

HELLO AND GOODBYE

Language	Hello or Good Day	Goodbye
Chinese ("Mandarin" dialect)	dzǎu	dzàijyàn
Danish	hallo	farvel
French	bon jour	au revoir
German	guten tag	auf Wiedersehen
Hawaiian	aloha	aloha
Hebrew	shalom	shalom
Italian	buon giorno	addio
Farsi (Iran)	salaam	khoda hafez
	سلام	خدا حافظ
Polish	hallo	żegnam
Portuguese	alô	adeus
Russian	Здравствуйте	до свидания
pronunciation	ZDRAHST-vooy-tyeh	daw svee-DA-nee-ya
Swahili	neno la kusalimu rafiki au mtani	kwa heri
Tagalog (Philippines)	kumusta	paalám
Spanish	holá	adiós
Swedish	god dag	adjö
Thai	sa wat dee ka	la kone na ka

SIGNS, SYMBOLS, TELESCOPES, & T-SQUARES

six
SIGNS & SYMBOLS

MATH SIGNS AND SYMBOLS

+	addition sign, plus, positive	∟	right angle
−	subtraction sign, minus, negative	∠	angle
±	plus or minus	r	radius
×	multiplication sign, multiplied by, times	d	diameter
÷	division sign, divided by	π	Pi, the number 3.1416
=	equals, is equal to	≅	congruent, is congruent to
≠	is not equal to	→	ray
<	less than	⊥	perpendicular, is perpendicular to
>	greater than	∥	parallel, is parallel to
≪	much less than	@	at
≫	much greater than	#	number or pound
$	dollar sign	%	percent
¢	cent(s)	°	degree(s)
£	pound sign used for monetary units (such as the Israeli and British pound)	∞	infinity
		:	is to, the ratio of
∷	as, equals	√	square root
∴	therefore	{}	indicates a set
∵	since, because	φ	empty set
△	triangle		
□	square		
▭	rectangle		

From *The Teacher's Book of Lists* © 1979, Goodyear Publishing Company, Inc.

HOBO SIGNS

Hobo signs are usually drawn with chalk on fences, sidewalks, trees, or poles to tell the next hobo passing by what to expect in a town or place.

KIND LADY LIVES HERE

VICIOUS DOG HERE

A GENTLEMAN LIVES HERE

THESE PEOPLE ARE RICH

WATCH OUT FOR THIEVES

YOU CAN SLEEP IN HAYLOFT

OR

TELL A SAD STORY

WOMAN LIVES HERE

YOU CAN GET FOOD HERE BY WORKING

OR

DOCTOR HERE, WON'T CHARGE

FREE TELEPHONE

JAIL

IF SICK, WILL CARE FOR YOU

KEEP QUIET

HOLD YOUR TONGUE

BARKING DOG HERE

BEWARE OF FOUR DOGS

YOU CAN CAMP HERE

DRINKING WATER, SAFE CAMP

DANGEROUS DRINKING WATER

O.K., ALL RIGHT

MAN WITH A GUN LIVES HERE

OPEN EYE, POLICE ARE LOOKING FOR HOBOES

CLOSED EYE, POLICE NOT LOOKING FOR HOBOES

NOTHING TO BE GAINED HERE

GOOD PLACE FOR A HANDOUT

TROLLEY STOP

GOOD PLACE TO CATCH A TRAIN

THIS IS NOT A SAFE PLACE

DANGER

NO USE GOING THIS DIRECTION

THIS WAY

HIT THE ROAD! QUICK! GO!

OR

HALT

DANGEROUS NEIGHBORHOOD

DISHONEST PERSON LIVES HERE

COWARDS, WILL GIVE, TO GET RID OF YOU

CRIME COMMITTED, NOT SAFE FOR STRANGERS

JUDGE LIVES HERE

COURTHOUSE; PRECINCT STATION

OFFICER OF LAW LIVES HERE

From *The Teacher's Book of Lists* © 1979, Goodyear Publishing Company, Inc.

HOBO SIGNS

1.   Draw a hobo sign on each object pictured below.
2.   Under each picture write the meaning of the signs you've drawn.
3.   On the back of this page, or on another sheet of paper, write a story telling what happened to cause a hobo to leave these signs.

X MARKS THE SPOT—X'S AND O'S

The X's and O's list can add to children's understanding that information can be communicated symbolically in many ways, including the use of letters. Children may wish to illustrate some of these symbolic meanings and collect examples of the use of X, O, and other letters from magazines, newspapers, and product packages and wrappings.

X's

multiplication sign; times
by, as in 4' x 4'
a tic tac toe sign
railroad crossing
marks a spot on a map
Roman numeral ten
as in brand X
closed lane
a vote
a way to sign your name if you don't know
  how to write
axis, used in mathematics
cross out
a kiss in a letter or note
an unknown amount

O's

oxygen
some highway markers
zero
a hug in a letter or note
some cities on maps
a tic tac toe sign
ceiling outlet on a blueprint
empty set (ϕ)

From *The Teacher's Book of Lists* © 1979, Goodyear Publishing Company, Inc.

COMIC STRIP SYMBOLS

Many ideas in comic strips are communicated without the use of words. Following are some common comic strip symbols and their usual meanings.

confused

unprintable

gloomy or sad

thinking

sleeping

words are coming from telephone, radio, or TV

an idea

in love

shivering from fright or cold

in a hurry

shiny or bright

hot or relieved

in a daze or something has been hit

From *The Teacher's Book of Lists* © 1979, Goodyear Publishing Company, Inc.

COMIC STRIP WORDS

AAAAGH	BZZ-ZT	OOOO-OH	WHAP
AAA-CHOO	CRACK	PHZZZ	WHOMP
AARGH	EEEYAAAA	POOF	WHOOSH
AH-HAAA	GLOM	POW	WHUMP
ARRGGG	HAH	SNIP	WOK
BANG	HA-HA-HA-HA-HA	SPLAM	YEOWW
BLAM	HISS	THUD	YYYYIIII
BOM	KER-PLOP	UGH	ZAK
BONG	KLINK	UNGAAA	ZAP
BONK	KWAM	UNGARRR	
BOO	KWOMP	WHAM	

COMIC STRIP FACIAL EXPRESSIONS

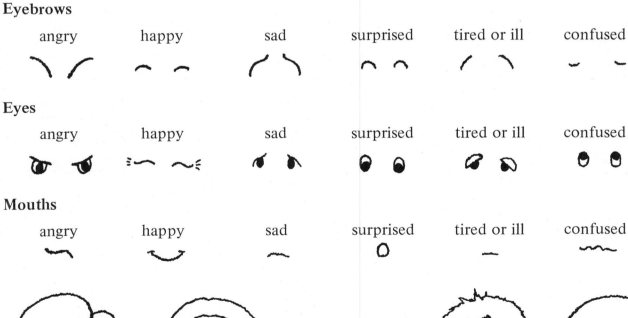

Eyebrows

angry   happy   sad   surprised   tired or ill   confused

Eyes

angry   happy   sad   surprised   tired or ill   confused

Mouths

angry   happy   sad   surprised   tired or ill   confused

angry

happy

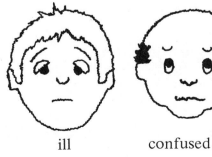

ill   confused

Comic Strip Activities

1. Draw a strip using only symbols, facial expressions, and comic strip words to communicate the story.

2. Select several comic strip words. Describe or illustrate situations in which they would be used.

3. Cut out examples from real comic strips to match any of the symbols, facial expressions, or comic strip words on the lists.

4. Cut out photographs of people or animals from newspapers and magazines. Label them with appropriate comic strip symbols or words.

5. Write an autobiography or biography of a cartoon character.

6. Keep a journal to summarize a strip day-by-day.

CHEMICAL SYMBOLS

"Dr. Strangebrain locked the door to his lab and stirred up the secret compound of two parts Uranium, one part Antimony, and three parts Lithium. He recorded the compound in his log:

"2U + 1Sb + 3Li."

A smattering of chemical names and symbols can add authentic-sounding details to children's stories of mad scientists and crazy chemists.

Actinium—Ac	Fermium—Fm	Neodymium—Nd	Samarium—Sm
Aluminum—Al	Fluorine—F	Neon—Ne	Scandium—Sc
Americium—Am	Francium—Fr	Neptunium—Np	Selenium—Se
Antimony—Sb	Gadolinium—Gd	Nickel—Ni	Silicon—Si
Argon—Ar	Gallium—Ga	Niobium	Silver—Ag
Arsenic—As	Germanium—Ge	(Columbium) Nb	Sodium—Na
Astatine—At	Gold—Au	Nitrogen—N	Strontium—Sr
Barium—Ba	Hafnium—Hf	Nobelium—No	Sulfur—S
Berkelium—Bk	Helium—He	Osmium—Os	Tantalum—Ta
Beryllium—Be	Holmium—Ho	Oxygen—O	Technetium—Tc
Bismuth—Bi	Hydrogen—H	Palladium—Pd	Tellurium—Te
Boron—B	Indium—In	Phosphorus—P	Terbium—Tb
Bromine—Br	Iodine—I	Platinum—Pt	Thallium—Tl
Cadmium—Cd	Iridium—In	Plutonium—Pu	Thorium—Th
Calcium—Ca	Iron—Fe	Polonium—Po	Thulium—Tm
Californium—Cf	Krypton—Kr	Potassium—K	Tin—Sn
Carbon—C	Lanthanum—La	Praseodymium—Pr	Titanium—Ti
Cerium—Ce	Lawrencium—Lr	Promethium—Pm	Tungsten (Wolfram)—W
Cesium—Cs	Lead—Pb	Protactinium—Pa	Uranium—U
Chlorine—Cl	Lithium—Li	Radium—Ra	Vanadium—V
Chromium—Cr	Lutetium—Lu	Radon—Rn	Xenon—Xe
Cobalt—Co	Magnesium—Mg	Rhenium—Re	Ytterbium—Yb
Copper—Cu	Manganese—Mn	Rhodium—Rh	Yttrium—Y
Curium—Cm	Mendelevium—Md	Rubidium—Rb	Zinc—Zn
Dysprosium—Dy	Mercury—Hg	Ruthenium—Ru	Zirconium—Zr
Einsteinium—Es	Molybdenum—Mo		
Erbium—Er			
Europium—Eu			

From The Teacher's Book of Lists © 1979, Goodyear Publishing Company, Inc.

INTERNATIONAL MORSE CODE

Samuel Morse telegraphed this message, "What hath God wrought."
Children can transmit their own messages, spelling words, and math
problems by tapping with a pencil or by using a telegraph (have your
mechanical wizard make one).

A	._	O	_ _ _	3	. . . _ _	
B	_...	P	._ _ .	4	. . . . _	
C	_._.	Q	_ _ . _	5	. . . . .	
D	_..	R	._.	6	_	
E	.	S	. . .	7	_ _ . . .	
F	. . _ .	T	_	8	_ _ _ . .	
G	_ _ .	U	. . _	9	_ _ _ _ .	
H	. . . .	V	. . . _	0	_ _ _ _ _	
I	. .	W	. _ _	Period	. _ . _ . _	
J	. _ _ _	X	_ . . _	Comma	_ _ . . _ _	
K	_ . _	Y	_ . _ _	Question Mark	. . _ _ . .	
L	. _ . .	Z	_ _ . .	Colon	_ _ _ . . .	
M	_ _	1	. _ _ _ _	Semicolon	_ . _ . _ .	
N	_ .	2	. . _ _ _	Quotation marks	. _ . . _ .	

Some brief forms often used in communications:

AR (end of message) . _ . _ .
EEEEEE (error) . . . .
A (affirmative-yes) . _
N (negative-no) _ .
R (message received and understood) . _ .
SOS (distress signal) . . . _ _ _ . . .

TIME OUT—IMPORTANT FOOTBALL AND BASKETBALL SIGNALS

Football

Offside

Illegal Procedure

Illegal Motion

Intentional Grounding

Unsportsmanlike Conduct

Clipping

Dead Ball

Touchdown or Field Goal

Personal Foul

Roughing the Kicker

Illegal Use of Hands and Arms

Time Out

First Down

Start the Clock

Safety

Illegally Passing or Handing Ball Forward

Forward Pass or Kick-Catching Interference

Ineligible Receiver Down Field on Pass

Ball Illegally Touched, Kicked, or Batted

Incomplete Forward Pass, Penalty Declined, No Play, or No Score

From *The Teacher's Book of Lists* © 1979, Goodyear Publishing Company, Inc.

Basketball

Personal Foul

Illegal Use of Hands

Pushing

Player Control Foul

Holding

Technical Foul

Traveling

Illegal Dribble

Cancel Score

Time Out

HAND ALPHABET

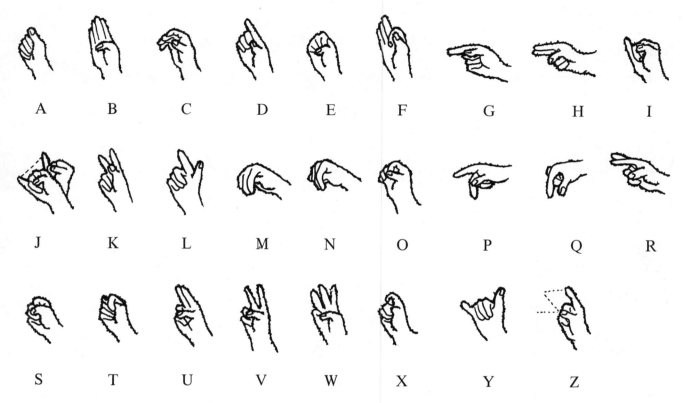

A B C D E F G H I

J K L M N O P Q R

S T U V W X Y Z

From The Teacher's Book of Lists © 1979, Goodyear Publishing Company, Inc.

WEATHER SYMBOLS

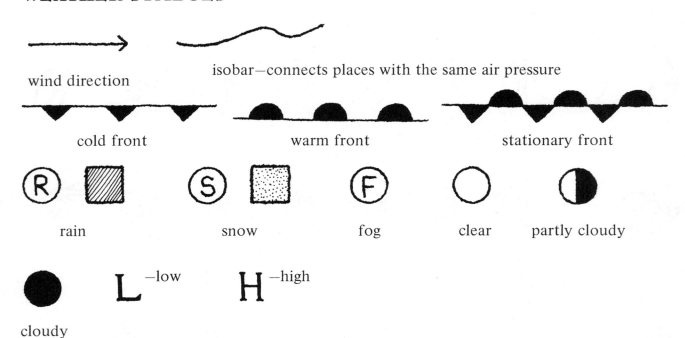

wind direction

isobar—connects places with the same air pressure

cold front

warm front

stationary front

rain

snow

fog

clear

partly cloudy

cloudy

L —low

H —high

Wind and cloud cover—tail points in the direction from which the wind is blowing.

clear;
wind 1–4 mph

clear;
wind 5–8 mph

clear;
wind 9–14 mph

clear;
wind 15–20 mph

partly cloudy;
wind 21–25 mph

partly cloudy;
wind 21–31 mph

partly cloudy;
wind 32–37 mph

completely cloudy;
wind 55–60 mph

completely cloudy;
wind 67–71 mph

hurricane

Name _____

WHAT'S THE WEATHER?

Directions: Read the weather report. Mark the map with weather symbols that go with the report. Draw three more weather symbols on the map and complete the weatherman's report for the symbols you've added.

A cold front is moving across Oregon bringing snow. Over Texas it is partly cloudy with winds of 23 mph blowing from the north. Southern California continues to be rainy. _____

OREGON

CALIFORNIA

TEXAS

From *The Teacher's Book of Lists* ©1979, Goodyear Publishing Company, Inc.

MAP SYMBOLS

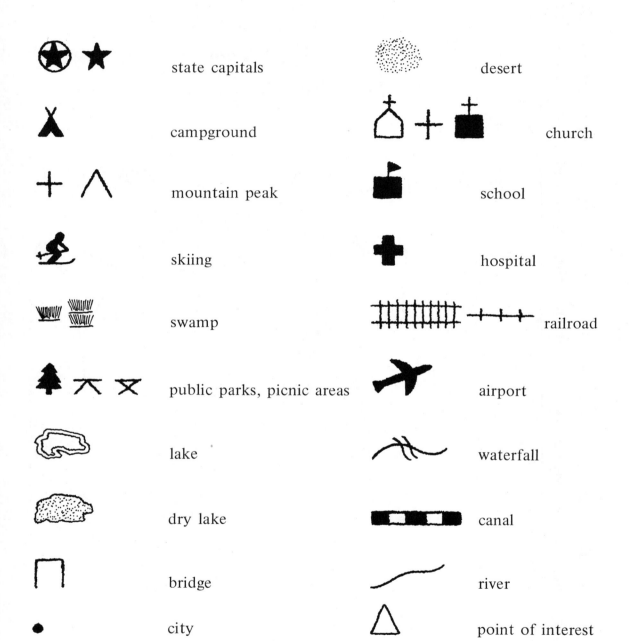

state capitals

campground

mountain peak

skiing

swamp

public parks, picnic areas

lake

dry lake

bridge

city

tunnel

desert

church

school

hospital

railroad

airport

waterfall

canal

river

point of interest

forest

Name _____

MAPMAKERS

Draw symbols on the map and make up a name for each. In the Map Index list each place name and the letter and number that shows its location.

	A	B	C	D	E	F	G	H
1								
2								
3								
4								
5								
6						⛺ Tall Pines Campground		
7								

MAP INDEX

Tall Pines Campground F6

From The Teacher's Book of Lists ©1979, Goodyear Publishing Company, Inc.

RED LIGHT/GREEN LIGHT—SYMBOLIC USES OF COLOR

Colors are often used to communicate meaning symbolically, without words. Here are some examples for red and green.

Red lights and their usual meanings:

Automobile brake lights—car is stopping or slowing down

Automobile dashboard—warning (brake is set, gas or oil is needed)

Doors or halls—exit here

Electrical appliances—appliance is on or hot

Railroads—stop

Traffic lights—stop

TV Studios—don't come in now (filming is in progress)

Vending machines—empty or out of a given item

Other uses of red:

Red flag at the beach—heavy, dangerous surf

Red letters or markings—flammable materials; fire-fighting equipment

Red ribbon—second place in a contest

Idioms based on red:

blood-red—having the deep-red color of blood

in the red—in debt

paint the town red—have an exciting time

red carpet treatment—extra-special treatment

red letter day—memorable or happy day

red tape—complicated procedure

sees red—is angry

Green lights and their usual meanings:

Railroads—track is clear

Traffic light—go

Other uses of green:

Green flag at the beach—average surf

Green flag in racing—start

Green power—ecology

Green letters or markings—safety

Idioms based on green:

greenbacks—paper currency

greenhorn—inexperienced person

green with envy or jealousy

green thumb—a talent for growing plants

green around the gills—sick

Activities For Red Light/Green Light

1. Make a priority list of the red lights and other red things in order from what is most important to what is least important for survival. Do the same for green.

2. Illustrate each of the idioms to show their literal meanings.

3. Add other colors and some of their symbolic meanings to the list.

From The Teacher's Book of Lists © 1979, Goodyear Publishing Company, Inc.

seven
TELESCOPES &
T-SQUARES

PLANET TABLE

The Planet Table can be the basis for many math activities. Older children can convert years to days, days to hours, hours to seconds, miles to kilometers, compute sums for each column, and make up problems for other children to solve. You may wish to round off some of the numbers to make them easier for children to work with.

	Average Distance From Sun (Miles)	Diameter (Miles)	Period of Revolution	Period of Rotation	Known Moons	Probable Temperature in °F	To Find Your Weight, Multiply Your Weight By:
Mercury	35,960,000	3,100	88 days	57 days	0	+600	0.27
Venus	67,200,000	7,700	225 days	247 days	0	+100	0.85
Earth	92,900,000	7,918	365¼ days	23 hrs 56 mins	1	+50	1.00
Mars	141,500,000	4,200	687 days	24 hrs 37 mins	2	+0	0.38
Jupiter	483,400,000	89,000	11.86 years	9 hrs 55 mins	13	−150	2.64
Saturn	886,200,000	71,500	29.5 years	10 hrs 14 mins	10	−250	1.17
Uranus	1,783,000,000	30,000	84 years	10 hrs 45 mins	5	−350	0.92
Neptune	2,790,000,000	27,700	164.75 years	15 hrs 45 mins	2	−400	1.12
Pluto	3,670,000,000	3,664	248.5 years	6.4 days	0	?	?

Planet Table Activities

1. Calculate what your weight would be on each planet.
2. Rewrite any or all of the columns in number words rather than numerals.

103

From The Teacher's Book of Lists © 1979, Goodyear Publishing Company, Inc.

3. Compute the differences between any two planets for each of the features shown on the table. Write statements to show your findings.

4. Design a travel brochure or poster for one of the planets. Use your imagination. It's okay to be unscientific.

FLY ME TO THE MOON—NOTABLE U.S. SPACE MISSIONS

Date	Mission	Crew	Duration (Hr:Min:Sec)	
May 5, 1961	Mercury-Redstone 3	Shepard	00:15:22	First American in space; a suborbital flight
Feb. 20, 1962	Mercury-Atlas 6	Glenn	04:55:23	First American in orbit; a three-orbit flight
June 3–7, 1965	Gemini-Titan IV	McDivitt, White	97:56:11	White becomes the first American to walk in space (20 minutes)
March 16, 1966	Gemini-Titan VIII	Armstrong, Scott	10:41:26	First docking of one space vehicle with another
June 3–6, 1966	Gemini-Titan IX-A	Stafford, Cernan	72:21:00	Cernan carried out 2 hours 7 minutes extravehicular activity
Sept. 12–15, 1966	Gemini-Titan XI	Conrad, Gordon	71:17:08	Gemini set a record altitude of 739.2 miles

Nov. 11–15, 1966	Gemini-Titan XII	Lovell, Aldrin	94:34:31	Final Gemini flight; Aldrin set a record total of 5 hours 30 minutes of extravehicular activity
Oct. 11–22, 1968	Apollo-Saturn 7	Schirra, Eisele, Cunningham	260:09:03	First manned flight of Apollo spacecraft
Dec. 21–27, 1968	Apollo-Saturn 8	Borman, Lovell, Anders	147:00:42	First flight to the moon; views of lunar surface televised to earth
March 3–13, 1969	Apollo-Saturn 9	McDivitt, Scott, Schweickart	241:00:54	First manned flight of lunar module
July 16–24, 1969	Apollo-Saturn 11	Armstrong, Collins, Aldrin	195:18:35	First lunar landing (in the Sea of Tranquility); lunar stay time 21:36:21; took lunar surface samples of 48.5 pounds
July 26–Aug. 7, 1971	Apollo-Saturn 15	Scott, Worden, Irwin	295:11:53	Fourth lunar landing; first use of lunar roving vehicle
Dec. 7–19, 1972	Apollo-Saturn 17	Cernan, Evans, Schmitt	301:51:59	Last Apollo flight to moon
May 25–June 22, 1973	Skylab 2	Conrad, Kerwin, Weitz	672:49:49 (28 days)	First U.S. manned orbiting space station mission
Nov. 16, 1973– Feb. 8, 1974	Skylab 4	Carr, Gibson, Pogue	2017:16:30 (84 days)	Final Skylab manned visit; longest flight of men in space; made observations of Comet Kohoutek; set record for space walk—7 hours, 1 minute
July 17, 1975 (Rendezvous and Docking)	Apollo-Soyuz Test Project	U.S.: Stafford, Brand, Slayton Russia: Leonov, Kubasov		First docking between U.S. and Russian spacecraft; cosmonauts and astronauts visited each other's spacecraft

The next major space mission will be the Space Shuttle, planned for 1980.

SOURCE: NASA

From *The Teacher's Book of Lists* © 1979, Goodyear Publishing Company, Inc.

A Dozen Debriefing Questions to be used with Fly Me to the Moon, p. 104 and 105.

1. Who was the first American to walk in space?

_____

2. Which was the first flight to the moon?

_____

3. What was the site of the first lunar landing?

_____

4. When did the first manned orbiting space station mission begin?

_____

5. During which mission did the first manned flight of the lunar module occur?

_____

6. Who were the astronauts who set a Gemini altitude record?

_____

7. Of the notable space missions listed, which was the longest Gemini flight? How much longer was it than the shortest Gemini flight?

_____

8. How much time did Scott spend in space according to the list?

_____

9. What notable space event occurred on July 17, 1975?

_____

10. What piece of equipment was used for the first time on the Apollo-Saturn 15 mission?

_____

11. What were the two notable missions Armstrong was on?

_____

12. Including the walks in space, what was the total time of extravehicular activity reported?

_____

SPACE TALK—SPACE TERMS USED IN AIR-TO-GROUND COMMUNICATION

Booster, bugs, foxtrot, footprints, and the Brooklyn Clothesline will become familiar words as children develop play and radio dialogues and reenactments of extraterrestrial travel based on the following Space Talk vocabulary. Children will want to make props, such as instrument panels and spacecraft models, incorporating items from the list.

ABORT—to cut short a mission or launch due to problems

ALL BALLS—flight crew slang for all zeroes

ALPHA—alphabet designation for the letter A

AMBIENT—the environmental condition, such as temperature, air pressure

APOGEE—the highest point in an orbit around earth

AUDIO SYSTEM—voice portion of communications system

BACKUP—item or system kept on hand to replace one that fails; astronaut or crew used to replace the prime crew in the event of illness

BARBER POLES—small gauges on control panels that are striped diagonally in black and white

BECO—booster engine cut-off

BLACKOUT—a fadeout of radio communication between a spacecraft and the ground during reentry

BLOCKHOUSE—Launch Control Center at Pad 39, Cape Kennedy

BOOSTER—launch vehicle

BRAVO—alphabet designation for the letter B

BREAKING UP—a garbling of voice transmission

BROOKLYN CLOTHESLINE—a loop of rope on pulleys used to transport film during extravehicular activities (EVAs)

BUG—an unidentified problem

BURN—the firing of engines

BUTTON UP—to completely close or seal any unit or vehicle such as the spacecraft

CHARLIE—alphabet designation for the letter C

CSM—COMMAND AND SERVICE MODULE—three-man spacecraft used in Apollo; same type of vehicle used to transport crews and equipment to and from Skylab

COMMAND MODULE—the crew portion of the CSM (see above definition)

COPY—synonym for read (understand, as during a voice transmission)

COUNTDOWN—step-by-step preparation for launch

From *The Teacher's Book of Lists* © 1979, Goodyear Publishing Company, Inc.

DAMPING—restraining; slowing down or stopping

DEBRIEFING—questioning of crewmen after a mission to obtain useful information

DEBUG—remove problems or malfunctions from a system

DELTA—alphabet designation for the letter D

DEORBIT—coming out of an earth orbit into splashdown trajectory

DOWN IN THE MUD—slang for very low volume in radio reception

DOWNTIME—time during which a system is not in condition or functioning

DRAG—resistance of the air to a body in motion

ECHO—alphabet designation for the letter E

EGRESS—to exit the spacecraft

EVA—extravehicular activity

FIVE BY FIVE—a term denoting radio reception is loud and clear

FOOTPRINT—the area of possible landing points for a vehicle at reentry

FOXTROT—alphabet designation for the letter F

GLITCH—a problem of any nature, especially during countdown

GOLF—alphabet designation for the letter G

HANDOVER—to pass spacecraft communication from one tracking station to another

HOLD—a delay in the launch countdown

HOTEL—alphabet designation for the letter H

INDIA—alphabet designation for the letter I

INGRESS—to enter the spacecraft

JETTISON—to discard into space

JULIET—alphabet designation for the letter J

KILO—alphabet designation for the letter K

LAUNCH VEHICLE—the booster as opposed to the spacecraft

LAUNCH WINDOW—the limited frame of time during which launch can be accomplished

LIMA—alphabet designation for the letter L

MIKE—alphabet designation for the letter M

MURPHY'S LAW—a so-called "scientific" law that states "What can go wrong will go wrong"

NO GO—indicates something is functioning improperly; not ready to proceed

NO JOY—slang meaning an expected event has not happened or a looked-for object has not been located

NOVEMBER—alphabet designation for the letter N

OPEN ENDED MISSION—a flight of no specific duration; continues as long as equipment functions properly

OSCAR—alphabet designation for the letter O

PAPA—alphabet designation for the letter P

PASS—the passage of a spacecraft over a tracking station or target area

PIGTAIL—a short, coiled wire or bundle of wires

POLL THE ROOM—take a consensus of flight controllers before making a go or no go decision

POO—Program Zero-Zero—clearing the spacecraft computer

POT—potable, drinkable

PUSH-TO-TALK—microphone switch which is pressed when a crewman wishes to transmit his voice

Q-BALL—device in nose cone of launch escape system which provides information

QUEBEC—alphabet designation for the letter Q

READ—understand, as during a voice transmission

REAL TIME—indicates the reporting of events at the nearly instantaneous time they occur

REV—revolution

ROGER—okay; will do

ROMEO—alphabet designation for the letter R

R & R—rest and recreation

SCRUB—to cancel or postpone a flight

SHOT—slang for launch or flight

SIERRA—alphabet designation for the letter S

SKIN TRACKING—tracking by radar bounced off the outside of the vehicle

SOM—start of message

SPLASHDOWN—impact of the spacecraft in the ocean during landing

TANGO—alphabet designation for the letter T

THRUST—push; force developed by a rocket engine

TOK—thrust O.K.

UNIFORM—alphabet designation for the letter U

VICTOR—alphabet designation for the letter V

WARMER—flight control slang for "better"

WHISKEY—alphabet designation for the letter W

WILCO—pilot slang for "will comply"

YANKEE—alphabet designation for the letter Y

ZIPS—all zeroes

ZULU—alphabet designation for the letter Z

From *The Teacher's Book of Lists* © 1979, Goodyear Publishing Company, Inc.

MEASUREMENT ABBREVIATIONS

Metric Abbreviations

nanometer—nm
millimeter—mm
centimeter—cm
decimeter—dm
meter—m
dekameter—dam
hectometer—hm
kilometer—km

milliliter—ml
centiliter—cl
deciliter—dl
liter—l
dekaliter—dal
hectoliter—hl
kiloliter—kl

milligram—mg
centigram—cg
decigram—dg
gram—g
dekagram—dag
hectogram—hg
kilogram—kg
metric ton—t

square millimeter—mm^2
square centimeter—cm^2
square meter—m^2
are—a
hectare—ha
square kilometer—km^2

cubic millimeter—mm^3
cubic centimeter—cm^3
cubic decimeter—dm^3
cubic meter—m^3

Other Measurement Abbreviations

inch—in, ″
foot—ft, ′
yard—yd
rod—rd
furlong—fur
mile—mi

gill—gi
pint—pt
quart—qt
gallon—gal

peck—pk
bushel—bu

chain—ch

cup—c
teaspoon—t, tsp
tablespoon—T, tbsp

grain—gr
pennyweight—dwt
ounce troy—oz t
pound troy—lb t

dram—dr
ounce—oz
pound—lb, #
hundredweight—cwt
ton—t

second—sec, ″
minute—min, ′
hour—hr
day—da
week—wk
month—mo
year—yr

barrel—bbl
cord—cd
fathom—fm

WEIGHTS AND MEASURES

Metric Weights and Measures

Length

10 millimeters = 1 centimeter
10 centimeters = 1 decimeter = 100 mm
10 decimeters = 1 meter   = 1000 mm
10 meters   = 1 dekameter
10 dekameters   = 1 hectometer = 100 m
10 hectometers = 1 kilometer = 1000 m

Liquid

10 milliliters = 1 centiliter
10 centiliters = 1 deciliter = 100 ml
10 deciliters   = 1 liter   = 1000 ml
10 liters   = 1 dekaliter
10 dekaliters   = 1 hectoliter = 100 liters
10 hectoliters = 1 kiloliter = 1000 liters

Liquid

8 drams   = 1 ounce
4 gills   = 1 pint   = 16 ounces
2 pints   = 1 quart   = 8 gills
4 quarts   = 1 gallon   = 8 pints = 32 gills
31½ gallons   = 1 barrel   = 126 quarts
2 barrels   = 1 hogshead = 63 gallons
                           = 252 quarts

Dry

2 pints   = 1 quart
8 quarts = 1 peck   = 16 pints
4 pecks   = 1 bushel = 32 quarts
                     = 64 pints
105 quarts = 1 barrel

Volume

1,728 cubic inches = 1 cubic foot
27 cubic feet   = 1 cubic yard
144 cubic inches   = 1 board foot
128 cubic feet   = 1 cord

Angular and Circular Measure

60 seconds = 1 minute
60 minutes = 1 degree
90 degrees = 1 quadrant
180 degrees = 1 straight angle
360 degrees = 1 circle = 4 quadrants

Length

12 inches = 1 foot
3 feet   = 1 yard
5½ yards = 1 rod, pole, or perch (16½ ft)
40 rods   = 1 furlong   = 220 yards
                            = 660 feet
8 furlongs = 1 statute mile = 1,760 yards
                            = 5,280 ft.
3 miles   = 1 league   = 5,280 yds.
                            = 15,840 ft.

Area

144 square inches = 1 square foot
9 square feet   = 1 square yard
                  = 9 sq. ft. = 1,296 sq. in.
30¼ square rods   = 1 sq. rod
                  = 272¼ sq. ft.
960 square rods   = 1 acre
                  = 4,840 sq. yds.
                  = 43,560 sq. ft.
1 square mile   = 640 acres
6 miles square   = 1 township
                  = 36 sections
                  = 36 square miles

Weight—Avoirdupois

27 11/32 grains	= 1 dram	
16 drams	= 1 ounce	= 437.5 grains
16 ounces	= 1 pound	= 256 drams
		= 7,000 grains
100 pounds	= 1 hundredweight	
20 hundredweights	= 1 ton	= 2,000 pounds
20 long hundredweights	= 1 long ton	= 2,240 pounds

Weight—Troy

24 grains	= 1 pennyweight	
20 pennyweights	= 1 ounce troy	= 480 grains
12 ounces troy	= 1 pound troy	
	= 240 pennyweights	
	= 5,760 grains	

Volume

1000 cubic millimeters	= 1 cubic centimeter	
1000 cubic centimeters	= 1 cubic decimeter	= 1,000,000 mm³
1000 cubic decimeters	= 1 cubic meter	
	= 1 stere	
	= 1,000,000 cm³	
	= 1,000,000,000 mm³	

Area

100 square millimeters	= 1 square centimeter
100 square centimeters	= 1 square decimeter
100 square decimeters	= 1 square meter = 10,000 cm² = 1,000,000 mm²
100 square meters	= 1 are
10 ares	= 1 hectare = 10,000 m²
100 hectares	= 1 square kilometer = 1,000,000 m²

Weight

10 milligrams	= 1 centigram	
10 centigrams	= 1 decigram	= 100 mg
10 decigrams	= 1 gram	= 1,000 mg
10 grams	= 1 dekagram	
10 dekagrams	= 1 hectogram	= 100 grams
10 hectograms	= 1 kilogram	= 1,000 grams
100 kilograms	= 1 quintal	
10 quintals	= 1 metric ton	= 1,000 kilograms

GEOMETRIC FORMULAS

To find the circumference of a

CIRCLE, multiply the diameter by pi (π).

$$c = \pi d$$

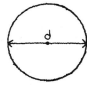

To find the perimeter of a

RECTANGLE, add twice the length to twice the width.

$$p = 2l + 2w$$

SQUARE, multiply the length of a side by 4.

$$p = 4s$$

TRIANGLE, add the length of the sides.

$p = a + b + c$

To find the area of a

CIRCLE, multiply the square of the radius by pi (π).

$A = \pi r^2$

SQUARE, square one side.

$A = s^2$ or $A = s \times s$

RECTANGLE, multiply the base by the height.

$A = bh$

TRIANGLE, multiply the base by the height and divide by 2.

$A = \frac{1}{2}bh$ or $A = \dfrac{bh}{2}$

PARALLELOGRAM, multiply the base by the height.

$A = bh$

TRAPEZOID, multiply the sum of the lengths of the parallel sides by the height and divide by 2.

$A = h \times \dfrac{b^1 + b^2}{2}$

ELLIPSE, multiply ½ the length of the major axis by ½ the length of the minor axis times pi (π).

$A = \pi \left(\tfrac{1}{2}M \times \tfrac{1}{2}m\right)$

REGULAR POLYGON, multiply ½ the apothem (the perpendicular from the center to one side) by the number of sides times the length of a side.

$A = \frac{1}{2}ans$ or $A = \frac{1}{2}ap$

SPHERE, multiply the radius squared by 4 times pi (π).

$A = 4\pi r^2$

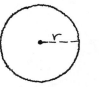

CYLINDER (lateral area or outside curved surface), multiply the diameter by the height times pi (π).

$A = \pi dh$

From The Teacher's Book of Lists © 1979, Goodyear Publishing Company, Inc.

To find the total area of a

CUBE, square the length of one edge and multiply by 6.
   $A = 6e^2$

RECTANGLE, add twice the product of the length and width, twice the product of the length and height, and twice the product of the width and height.
   $A = 2lw + 2lh + 2wh$ or $A = 2(lw + lh + wh)$

CYLINDER, add the lateral area to the area of the two bases.
   $A = \pi dh + 2\pi r^2$

To find the volume of a

CUBE, cube the length of one side.
   $V = s^3$

RECTANGULAR SOLID, multiply the length by the width times the height.
   $V = lwh$

CONE, multiply the square of the radius of the base by the height times $\frac{1}{3}$ pi (π)
   $V = \frac{1}{3}\pi r^2 h$

CYLINDER, multiply the square of the radius by the height times pi (π).
   $V = \pi r^2 h$

SPHERE, multiply the cube of the radius by $\frac{4}{3}$ pi (π).
   $V = \frac{4}{3}\pi r^3$

PYRAMID, multiply the area of the base by $\frac{1}{3}$ times the height.
   $V = \frac{1}{3}bh$

99 THINGS TO GRAPH AND SURVEY

Questions to ask for surveying and graphing

"How many . . . ?"

. . . people in your family
. . . rooms in your house
. . . light bulbs in your house
. . . cars in your family
. . . plants in your house
. . . televisions in your house
. . . electrical appliances in your house
. . . doors in your house

. . . windows in your house
. . . teeth do you have
. . . buttons do you have on
. . . pockets on what you're wearing
. . . relatives do you have
. . . letters in your name
. . . left- and right-handed people in your class

"At what time . . . ?"

. . . do you eat dinner
. . . do you get up
. . . do you go to bed
. . . do you leave for school

. . . do you get home from school
. . . is your favorite TV show on
. . . were you born

"How much time in a day or week do you spend . . . ?"

. . . watching television
. . . doing homework
. . . playing
. . . reading
. . . in a car or on a bus

. . . eating
. . . doing chores
. . . alone
. . . in activities such as Boy Scouts, Girl Scouts, piano lessons, etc.

"Who's your favorite . . . . ?"

. . . movie star
. . . TV star
. . . recording group
. . . book character

. . . sportsperson
. . . singer
. . . celebrity

"What's your favorite . . . . . . ?"

. . . ice cream flavor	. . . holiday	. . . book
. . . color	. . . film	. . . animal
. . . TV program	. . . radio station	. . . building
. . . kind of car	. . . food	. . . toy
. . . game or sport	. . . song	. . . musical instrument
. . . pet	. . . number	. . . pizza topping
. . . weather	. . . brand of jeans	

"How many times in a day or week . . . ?"

. . . do you use the telephone
. . . do you drink water
. . . does the telephone ring

"How old do you think our teacher is?"
"What do you want to be when you grow up?"
"In which month were you born?"
"What is your zodiac sign?"
"Where do you shop for groceries?"
"How much is your weekly allowance?"
"What is the first number of your telephone number?"
"What is the last number of your telephone number?"
"How many times can you jump on one foot?"
"How many sit-ups (jumping jacks, push-ups, etc.) can you do?"
"How long can you talk (filibuster)?"
"How many times can you jump rope without missing?"
"How many times can you say 'toyboat' clearly and quickly?"

The following ideas for graphing require observation or measurement of other people and things.

Within a given population or area, graph the color of:

eyes	cars
hair	flowers
shoes	books
articles of clothing	

Measure and graph people's:

heights

weights

length of arms, legs, or feet

circumference of heads

The following graphs generally can be done without interaction with other people.

Do weekly graphs of:

where people are eating lunch

students present or absent in class

the highest temperature for each day

the lowest temperature for each day

Do graphs at home of:

the kinds of silverware in a drawer

the kinds of dishes on a shelf

articles of clothing in a drawer or closet

types of TV commercials seen in an evening (cars, foods, cleaning products, etc.)

. . . And Other Things to Count and Graph

Choose a paragraph. Count and graph the number of times each letter of the alphabet appears in the paragraph.

Count and graph the number and kinds of P.E. equipment in your school.

Count and graph the number and kinds of supplies in your classroom (scissors, pencils, rulers, etc.).

Measure and graph the areas of all the rooms in your school.

Count and graph the number of times common names, such as Smith, Jones, Brown, White, Taylor, Johnson, Nelson, and Martin, appear in your telephone directory.

Count and graph the number of people in your class who have used each type of transportation: bus, airplane, taxi, ferry, train, horse, etc.

PEOPLE AND ANIMALS

From *The Teacher's Book of Lists* © 1979, Goodyear Publishing Company, Inc.

eight
PEOPLE

"HAIL TO THE CHIEF"—U.S. PRESIDENTS

President	Date of Birth	Date of Death	Date of Inauguration
George Washington	Feb. 22, 1732	Dec. 14, 1799	Apr. 30, 1789
John Adams	Oct. 30, 1735	July 4, 1826	Mar. 4, 1797*
Thomas Jefferson	Apr. 13, 1743	July 4, 1826	1801
James Madison	Mar. 16, 1751	June 28, 1836	1809
James Monroe	Apr. 28, 1758	July 4, 1831	1817
John Quincy Adams	July 11, 1767	Feb. 23, 1848	1825
Andrew Jackson	Mar. 15, 1767	June 8, 1845	1829
Martin Van Buren	Dec. 5, 1782	July 24, 1862	1837
William Henry Harrison	Feb. 9, 1773	Apr. 4, 1841	1841
John Tyler	Mar. 29, 1790	Jan. 18, 1862	1841 (April 6, after Harrison's death)
James Knox Polk	Nov. 2, 1795	June 15, 1849	1845
Zachary Taylor	Nov. 24, 1784	July 9, 1850	1849 (March 5)
Millard Fillmore	Jan. 7, 1800	Mar. 8, 1874	1850 (July 10, after Taylor's death)
Franklin Pierce	Nov. 23, 1804	Oct. 8, 1869	1853
James Buchanan	Apr. 23, 1791	June 1, 1868	1857
Abraham Lincoln	Feb. 12, 1809	Apr. 15, 1865	1861
Andrew Johnson	Dec. 29, 1808	July 31, 1875	1865 (April 15, after Lincoln's death)

Ulysses S. Grant	Apr. 27, 1822	July 23, 1885	1869
Rutherford B. Hayes	Oct. 4, 1822	Jan. 17, 1893	1877
James A. Garfield	Nov. 19, 1831	Sept. 19, 1881	1881
Chester A. Arthur	Oct. 5, 1829	Nov. 18, 1886	1881 (Sept. 20, after Garfield's death)
Grover Cleveland	Mar. 18, 1837	June 24, 1908	1885
Benjamin Harrison	Aug. 20, 1833	Mar. 13, 1901	1889
Grover Cleveland	Mar. 18, 1837	June 24, 1908	1893
William McKinley	Jan. 29, 1843	Sept. 14, 1901	1897
Theodore Roosevelt	Oct. 27, 1858	Jan. 6, 1919	1901 (Sept. 14, after McKinley's death
William H. Taft	Sept. 15, 1857	Mar. 8, 1930	1909
Woodrow Wilson	Dec. 28, 1856	Feb. 3, 1924	1913
Warren G. Harding	Nov. 2, 1865	Aug. 2, 1923	1921
Calvin Coolidge	July 4, 1872	Jan. 5, 1933	1923 (Aug. 3, after Harding's death)
Herbert Hoover	Aug. 10, 1874	Oct. 20, 1964	1929
Franklin D. Roosevelt	Jan. 30, 1882	Apr. 12, 1945	1933
Harry S. Truman	May 8, 1884	Dec. 26, 1972	1945 (April 12, after Roosevelt's death)
Dwight D. Eisenhower	Oct. 14, 1890	Mar. 28, 1969	Jan. 20, 1953
John F. Kennedy	May 29, 1917	Nov. 22, 1963	Jan. 20, 1961
Lyndon B. Johnson	Aug. 27, 1908	Jan. 22, 1973	Nov. 22, 1963 (after Kennedy's death)
Richard M. Nixon	Jan. 9, 1913		Jan. 20, 1969
Gerald R. Ford	July 14, 1913		Aug. 9, 1974
Jimmy Carter	Oct. 1, 1924		Jan. 20, 1977

*The following inaugurations were also on Mar. 4—through 1933, unless otherwise noted.

Presidential Activities

1. Make a list of the Presidents' ages when they died. (Pay special attention to the months.)
2. Make a list of the Presidents' ages when they were inaugurated. (Pay special attention to the months.)
3. Rearrange the list of Presidents to read in alphabetical order.

4. Group the Presidents according to the months in which they were born or died.

5. Group the Presidents according to the number of terms to which they were elected.

6. Make a list of facts—such as the President with the longest life, shortest life, shortest term of office, longest term of office, youngest to become President, and oldest to become President.

7. Add other columns to the chart, such as Vice-Presidents, previous professions or occupations, and party affiliations.

8. Do research to find out about:

    a. world events that occurred during a President's term of office;
    b. important legislation passed during a President's term of office;
    c. a President's early life.

WOMEN

This is a representative list of women who have made contributions in various fields.

Jane Addams—American social worker and humanitarian

Louisa May Alcott—American writer; author of *Little Women*

Judith Anderson—stage actress

Marian Anderson—American opera singer; first black to sing with the Metropolitan Opera Company

Susan B. Anthony—reformer and leader in the American women's suffrage movement

Joan Baez—American folk singer; active in antiwar and civil rights movements of the 1960s

Sirimavo Bandaranaike—world's first female prime minister (of Sri Lanka)

Romana Acosta Bañuelos—treasurer of the U.S., 1971–1974

Clara Barton—founded the American Red Cross

Simone de Beauvoir—French author

Catharine Beecher—early supporter of education for women

Patty Berg—a top tournament winner in women's golf

Sarah Bernhardt—American actress

Mary McLeod Bethune—American educator who worked to improve educational opportunities for blacks

Nellie Bly (Elizabeth Cochrane Seaman)—American journalist

Evangeline Booth—first woman to become international leader and general of the Salvation Army

Belle Boyd—Confederate spy

Sophonisba Breckinridge—pioneer teacher of Social Work

Emily Brontë—English novelist

Elizabeth Barrett Browning—a poet of Victorian England

Pearl S. Buck—American author

St. Frances Xavier Cabrini—first (naturalized) U.S. citizen to become a saint

Calamity Jane (Martha Jane Canary)—American frontierswoman

Mary Steichen Calderone—American physician

Maria Callas—American operatic soprano

Rachel Carson—American marine biologist and science writer

Mary Cassatt—American painter

Carrie Chapman Catt—American leader in the campaign for woman suffrage; founded what has become the League of Women Voters

Chicang Ch'ing—wife of Mao Tse-tung; became Chinese leader after Mao's death for a brief period

Shirley Chisholm—first black woman in U.S. Congress; campaigned for 1972 Presidential nomination

Jacqueline Cochran—American businesswoman and pioneer airplane pilot

Colette (Sidonie Gabrielle Claudine)—French author

Charlotte Corday—French patriot during the French Revolution

Marie Curie—Nobel Prize winning French physicist

Bette Davis—American motion-picture actress

Paulina Davis—American social reformer for women's rights

Agnes De Mille—American choreographer, dancer, and author

Bernadette Devlin—civil rights leader of the Roman Catholic minority in Northern Ireland

Babe Didrikson—one of the greatest of woman athletes

Dorothea Dix—led movement to build state hospitals for the mentally ill in the U.S.

Daphne du Maurier—British novelist

Isadora Duncan—greatly influential in the American dance of the early 1900s

Jacqueline du Pré—English cellist

Amelia Earhart—American aviator, writer, and lecturer; one of the first women pilots in the U.S.

Mary Baker Eddy—founder of Christian Science and the Church of Christ, Scientists

George Eliot (Mary Ann Evans)—great English novelist

Edna Ferber—American novelist and playwright

Margot Fonteyn—great English ballerina

Betty Friedan—American author and one of the founders of women's liberation movement

Indira Gandhi—first woman prime minister of India

Judy Garland—American singer and motion-picture actress

Emma Goldman—came to the U.S. from Russia; lectured in favor of anarchism and women's rights

Martha Graham—American pioneer of modern dance; dancer and choreographer

Ella T. Grasso—first woman elected governor in the U.S. who did not succeed her husband in the office

Kate Greenaway—English illustrator of children's books

Angelina and Sara Grimké—sisters who became abolitionists and pioneers in the U.S. women's rights movement

Alice Hamilton—American physician; did pioneer work in industrial medicine

Patricia Roberts Harris—first black woman to serve as U.S. ambassador

Helen Hayes—American stage and screen actress

Lillian Hellman—American playwright

Carla Anderson Hills—Secretary of Housing and Urban Development under President Ford

Billie Holiday—American jazz singer

Julia Ward Howe—American writer, lecturer, social reformer

Helen Hunt Jackson—worked for American Indian rights

Irène Joliot-Curie—Nobel Prize winner for chemistry; Marie Curie's daughter

Helen Keller—overcame physical handicaps (unable to see and hear) to become internationally famous; helped thousands of handicapped persons lead fuller lives

Elizabeth Kenny (Sister Kenny)—Australian nurse who developed a special method of treating polio

Billie Jean King—American tennis star

Selma Lagerlöf—Swedish writer; won the Nobel prize for literature in 1909

Lotte Lehmann—German soprano

Belva Lockwood—American reformer and women's suffrage leader

Juliette Gordon Low—founded the Girl Scouts in America

Amy Lowell—American poet and critic

Clare Boothe Luce—first woman to represent the U.S. in a major diplomatic post

Mary McCarthy—American author

Carson McCullers—American novelist

Golda Meir—prime minister of Israel, 1969–1974

Edna St. Vincent Millay—American poet

Marianne Moore—American poet

Grandma Moses (Anna Mary Roberson Moses)—American primitive painter

Lucretia Mott—American reformer; worked for women's rights and the abolition of slavery

Carry Amelia Moore Nation—crusaded against the use of alcoholic beverages

Florence Nightingale—founder of the modern nursing profession

Annie Oakley—American markswoman

Georgia O'Keeffe—American artist

Ruth Bryan Owen—first American woman to represent the U.S. in a foreign country

Vijaya Lakshmi Pandit—Indian woman famous for work in government and the women's movement

Dorothy Parker—American poet and writer of short stories and literary criticism

Frances Perkins—first woman cabinet member of the U.S.

Mary Pickford—American movie actress and producer

Sylvia Plath—American poet

Katherine Anne Porter—American writer, famous for her short stories

Leontyne Price—American operatic soprano

Jeannette Rankin—first woman elected to the U.S. Congress

Mary Roberts Rinehart—American novelist and playwright

Eleanor Roosevelt—wife of Franklin Delano Roosevelt; she became prominent in her own right for her humanitarian work

Nellie Tayloe Ross—first woman governor of the U.S.

Ruth Saint Denis—American dancer, teacher, and choreographer

George Sand (Amantine Dupin)—French novelist

Dorothy Sayers—English author, famous for detective stories

Elizabeth Ann Seton—first native-born person in the U.S. to be recognized as a saint

Beverly Sills—American opera singer

Gertrude Stein—American author

Gloria Steinem—American writer and leading supporter of women's liberation movement

Harriet Beecher Stowe—American novelist and writer

Joan Sutherland—Australian operatic soprano

Maria Tallchief—American ballerina

Helen Brooke Taussig—American physician specializing in children's heart diseases; discovered the cause of bluish tinge in skin of "blue babies"

Balentina Vladimirova Tereshkova—Russian woman who became the first woman to travel in space

Margaret Thatcher—first woman to head a British political party

Sojourner Truth (Isabella Baumfree)—American abolitionist; first black woman orator to speak out against slavery

Harriet Tubman—black American who helped hundreds of slaves escape to freedom; most famous leader of the underground railroad

Sigrid Undset—Norwegian author

Jane Goodall-Van Lawick—English zoologist; became famous for behavior studies of chimpanzees

Laura Ingalls Wilder—American author of children's books

Emma Willard—first American woman to lead movement for higher education for women

Frances E. Willard—American educator and social reformer

Victoria C. Woodhull—first woman to run for President of the U.S.

EXPLORERS AND DISCOVERERS

c. 1000	Leif Ericson	Thought to be the first European to reach North American mainland
1487–1488	Bartolomeu Dias	First European to sail around the Cape of Good Hope in Africa
1492–1504	Christopher Columbus	Made voyages to West Indies and Caribbean Islands
1497–1498	John Cabot	Made voyages across the Atlantic to the Canadian coast
1498	Vasco da Gama	First European to reach India by sea (sailed around Africa)
1497–1503	Amerigo Vespucci	Made voyages to West Indies and South America
1513	Vasco Núñez de Balboa	Crossed Isthmus of Panama; sighted Pacific Ocean
1513	Juan Ponce de León	Explored Florida
1519–1521	Hernando Cortes	Explored and conquered Mexico
1519–1521	Ferdinand Magellan	Led first voyage around the world; proved the world is round
1524	Giovanni da Verrazano	Explored Atlantic coast of the Americas while searching for a Northwest Passage

1531–1535	Francisco Pizarro	Explored and conquered Peru
1535	Jacques Cartier	Discovered and sailed up St. Lawrence River
1539–1542	Hernando de Soto	Explored Southeastern U.S.; reached Mississippi River
1540–1542	Francisco V. de Coronado	Explored Southwestern U.S., as far as central Kansas
1541	Francisco de Orellana	Explored Amazon River
1577–1580	Sir Francis Drake	First Englishman to sail around the world; explored California coast
1603–1616	Samuel de Champlain	Explored eastern coast of North America and St. Lawrence River
1609–1611	Henry Hudson	Explored Hudson Bay and River area
1673	Louis Joliet and Jacques Marquette	Explored northern Mississippi River basin
1727–1729	Vitus Bering	Explored Bering Strait; discovered Alaska
1768–1779	James Cook	Made extensive explorative voyages in the South Pacific
1789–1793	Sir Alexander Mackenzie	Explored western Canada
1804–1806	William Clark and Meriwether Lewis	Led expedition across the Rocky Mountains to the Pacific Ocean and back
1842–1846	John Charles Frémont	Explored extensively in western U.S.
1849–1873	David Livingstone	Greatest European explorer of Africa
1853–1858	Sir Richard Burton	Explored Arabia and East Africa
1874–1889	Sir Henry Stanley	Proved the source of the Nile; explored Congo River
1909	Robert Peary	Led the first expedition that reached the North Pole
1911	Roald Amundsen	First to reach the South Pole
1926–1929	Richard E. Byrd	Flew over both the North and South Poles; led five expeditions into the Antarctic
1957–1958	Sir Vivian Fuchs	Led first expedition across Antarctica

INVENTIONS AND INVENTORS

Thomas Edison is said to be the greatest of all the inventors in history. Among his many inventions and developments (he received 1,093 patents) are the electric light, a mimeograph machine, a motion-picture camera and projector, and the phonograph. We selected the following inventions because they are familiar products known by most children.

airplane, the first successful—Orville and Wilbur Wright   1903

aspirin—Dresser   1889

bakelite—one of the first plastics—L. H. Baekeland   1907

balloons that carry people in the air—Montgolfier   1783

bicycle, modern type—James Starley   1884

bifocal lens—Benjamin Franklin   1780

carpet sweeper—Bissell   1876

cellophane—J. E. Brandenberger   1912

clock, pendulum type—Christian Huygens   1657

dynamite—Alfred Nobel   1866

elevator, power type—Elisha Otis   1852

food preservation, by canning—Appert   1810

food preservation, by freezing—Clarence Birdseye   1920s

helicopter—Igor Sikorsky   1939

hydroplane—Glenn Curtiss   1911

kodak, roll-film hand camera—Eastman and Walker   1888

lawn mower—A. M. Hills   1868

lightning rod—Benjamin Franklin   1752

locomotive, first successful steam—George Stephenson   1829

mason jar—J. Mason   1858

matches, friction—John Walker   1827

microphone—Emil Berliner   1877

microscope, compound—Zacharias Janssen   1590

nylon—E. I. du Pont de Nemours & Co.   1937

oleomargarine—H. Mege-Mouries   1869

pen, first successful fountain—L. E. Waterman   1884

penicillin—Alexander Fleming   1929

phonograph—Thomas Edison   1877

piano—Bartollomeo Cristofori   1709

polio vaccines—Jonas Salk (1953) and Albert Sabin (1955)

printing from movable type—Johann Gutenberg   1450

rabies vaccine—Louis Pasteur   1885

radar—A. Hoyt Taylor and Leo C. Young   1922

razor, safety—Gillette   1895; electric—Schick   1931

refrigerating machine—John Gorie   1851

revolver—Samuel Colt   1835

sewing machine—Elias Howe   1846

From *The Teacher's Book of Lists* © 1979, Goodyear Publishing Company, Inc.

telegraph—Samuel Morse   1837

telephone—Alexander Graham Bell   1876

television—J. L. Baird 1925; independently by C. F. Jenkins   1925

thermometer—Galileo   1593; mercury thermometer—Gabriel Fahrenheit   1714

typewriter, first practicable—C. L. Sholes 1865

vacuum bottle—James Dewar   1893

vulcanization of rubber, a process that made rubber useful by giving it elasticity, hardness, and strength—Charles Goodyear   1844

x-ray—Wilhelm Roentgen   1895

zipper—Judson   1891

AWARDS FOR STUDENTS

Everybody likes recognition, so end your year with an Awards Day. Here's a list of awards that may match some of the personalities in your class. Obviously, some of the awards are stated with tongue in cheek, and need to be given and received with a sense of humor. The important thing is that everyone gets an award.

THE CHEERLEADER AWARD to the most enthusiastic

THE CHESHIRE CAT AWARD to the person with the biggest smile

THE NEATEST DESK or CUBBY AWARD

THE CALLIGRAPHY AWARD to the person with the neatest handwriting

THE VAN GOGH AWARD to the best artist

THE MOST HELPFUL AWARD

THE DR. FEELGOOD AWARD to the person with the best attendance

THE THESAURUS AWARD to the person with the biggest vocabulary.

THE FUNK AND WAGNALL AWARD to the best speller

THE FASHION PLATE AWARD to the best dressed

THE PHILANTHROPIC AWARD to the most generous

THE UMP AWARD to the best referee

THE SPIC AND SPAN AWARD to the best cleaner-upper

THE BEST SECRETARY AWARD

THE BEST EXCUSE-MAKER AWARD

THE MOST LOQUACIOUS AWARD

THE LADY GODIVA AWARD to the person with the longest hair

THE LONGEST LEGS AWARD

THE LITERARY AWARD to the person who has read the most books

THE BETTER-LATE-THAN-NEVER AWARD

THE ATHLETE AWARD

THE "I DIDN'T DO IT" AWARD to the person who is good at denying things

THE LOST AND FOUND AWARD to the person who is always losing things

THE "WE TRY HARDER" AWARD

THE STICK WITH IT AWARD to the person who stays with a task

THE SOFTEST-SPOKEN AWARD

THE LOUDEST-SPOKEN AWARD

THE HERMES AWARD to the best messenger

THE DO-RE-MI AWARD to the best singer

THE DEAN OF THE DISCOS AWARD to the best dancer

THE STAND-UP COMIC AWARD to the best joke teller

THE BIGGEST NAGGER AWARD

THE EASY-GOING AWARD to the most agreeable

THE BULL IN THE CHINA SHOP AWARD to the clumsiest

THE IMPOUND AWARD to the person who has lost the most stuff to the teacher's desk

THE BEST AFTER-SCHOOL TEACHER'S CAR LOADER or UNLOADER

THE TURTLE AWARD to the person who gets things done slowly

THE ALBERT EINSTEIN AWARD for outstanding achievement in science

THE ALWAYS ROOM FOR ONE MORE AWARD to the person with the fullest desk or cubby

THE NUMERO UNO AWARD to the best mathematician

THE "I'LL DO IT" AWARD to the person who volunteers the most

THE KVETCH AWARD to the biggest complainer

THE WORK IS NOT GOOD FOR MY HEALTH AWARD to the person who tries to avoid all assignments

THE EXTRA CREDIT AWARD

THE SIDE-BY-SIDE AWARD to two people who are inseparable

THE PEACEMAKER AWARD

THE GIGGLER AWARD

THE "I'D RATHER DO IT MYSELF" AWARD to the most independent

THE MOST SERIOUS AWARD

THE MOST IMPROVED AWARD

PEOPLE CELEBRATE—ETHNIC HOLIDAYS

Although some of the holidays on this list are celebrated by many Americans, we have listed the ethnic group for which the holiday holds special significance. Religious holidays have generally been omitted.

Date	Name	Ethnic Group	
January 15	Martin Luther King, Jr. Day	Black American	Commemorates the birthday of Martin Luther King, Jr., civil rights leader.
Observed between Jan. 21 & Feb. 19	Chinese New Year's	Chinese	Celebration lasts several days, ending with festivities that include a parade featuring the Golden Dragon, gongs, drums, and firecrackers.
February 4	Kosciuszko Day	Polish	Honors the birthday of Tadeusz Kosciuszko, who fought with the colonists in the American Revolutionary War.
March 3	Hina Matsuri (Girl's Day)	Japanese	Festival honoring girls and their dolls. Traditional dolls are displayed in the home.

From *The Teacher's Book of Lists* © 1979, Goodyear Publishing Company, Inc.

March 17	St. Patrick's Day	Irish	Feast day of St. Patrick, patron saint of Ireland. Celebrated with parades, balls, dinners.
March–April (date varies)	Pesach (Passover)	Jewish	Feast of unleavened bread. Commemorates the deliverance of the Jews from Egypt; observed for eight days.
May 5	Cinco de Mayo	Mexican	Commemorates the defeat of the French at the Battle of Puebla in 1867. Celebrated with a fiesta.
May 5	Tango No Sekku (Boy's Day)	Japanese	Festival honoring boys. Carp kites symbolizing strength and determination are flown from rooftops.
May 17	Syttende Mai	Norwegian	Celebrates the adoption of the Norwegian constitution in 1814.
June 24	Swedish Midsummer Festival	Swedish	Celebrated with dancing and the raising of the maypole.
July 29	Olsok Eve Festival (frequently called Norway Day in U.S.)	Norwegian	Commemorates the death of St. Olaf, the martyr king Olav Haraldsson who brought Christianity to Norway.
Setpember 27 (observed on the 4th Friday of September)	American Indian Day	American Indian	Honors native Americans.
September 28	Cabrillo Day	Portuguese	Six-day festival observed in California honoring Juan Rodriguez Cabrillo, Portuguese navigator who discovered California on September 28, 1542.
September (date varies)	Rosh Hashanah	Jewish	Jewish New Year
October 9	Leif Ericson Day	Norwegian & Icelandic	Commemorates the landing of Norsemen in Vinland, New England about A.D. 1000.
October 11	Pulaski Memorial Day	Polish	Commemorates the death of General Casimir Pulaski, hero of the American Revolution.
October 12 (observed on 2nd Monday of October)	Columbus Day	Italian	Commemorates the sighting of San Salvador on October 12, 1492, by Christopher Columbus.

BUTCHER, BAKER, CANDLESTICK MAKER—PEOPLE'S JOBS

A   acrobat, actor, aircraft worker, airline worker, architect, artist, assembler, astrologer, athlete, attorney, auctioneer, auto mechanic

B   babysitter, baker, banker, bank teller, bartender, beautician, beekeeper, biologist, bookkeeper, brick mason, broadcaster, bus driver, butcher, buyer

C   cake decorator, calligrapher, carpenter, cashier, chauffeur, chef, chemist, choreographer, clerk, computer programmer, contractor, construction worker, controller, cook

D   dancer, data processor, dental hygienist, dentist, dermatologist, designer, dietician, disc jockey, draftsperson, drummer

E   ecologist, economist, editor, electrician, engineer, engraver, entertainer, estimator

F   factory worker, farmer, file clerk, filmmaker, fireman, fisherman, florist, fortune teller

G   gardener, genealogist, geologist, ghost writer, golfer, graphic artist, grocer, guard

H   hair stylist, handyman, horse trainer, hypnotist

I   ice skater, illustrator, innkeeper, inspector, instructor, insurance agent, interior decorator, interpreter, inventor, inventory control clerk, investigator

J   janitor, jeweler, judge

K   keypunch operator

L   laboratory technician, legal secretary, librarian, linguist, lithographer, loan officer, locksmith

M   machinist, mail carrier, manager, manicurist, masseur or masseuse, mechanic, medical assistant, metallurgist, meteorologist, milliner, model, musician

N   news reporter, numismatist, nurse, nurseryman

O   occupational therapist, oil worker, optometrist, order clerk, organist

P   painter, personnel worker, pharmacist, photographer, physical therapist, physician, piano tuner, pilot, plasterer, plumber, police officer, printer, purchasing agent

Q   quality control manager, quilt maker

R   railroad worker, rancher, realtor, receptionist, recreation director, refinisher, repair person, restaurateur, roofer

S   salesperson, scuba diver, seamstress, secretary, service man or woman (Army, Navy, etc.), shipping clerk, sign painter, social worker, stenographer, steward or stewardess, surveyor

T   tailor, tattooer, taxidermist, taxi driver, teacher, telephone operator, therapist, tool and die maker, travel agent, truck driver, typesetter, typist

U   undertaker, upholsterer, urban planner

V   valet, veterinarian, video technician

W   waiter or waitress, warehouse person, watchmaker, welder, winemaker, writer

X   Xerox operator, x-ray technician, xmas tree grower

Y   yoga instructor

Z   zoologist

Activities With People's Jobs

1.   Write verbs to describe what each worker does.

2.   Use the workers listed in one letter category for the characters in a story. Some examples of titles are: "The Butler Did It," using the workers in the B list, and "The Plumber's Helpers," using the workers in the P list as characters.

3.   List the workers within general categories, such as Office, Entertainment, Industry, or Workers Who Come to Your Home.

4.   Choose one or more of the following "Planned Communities" and list all the workers who might live there: Beauty Burg, Fix-it Ville, Healthy Hamlet, Food Farm, Sports Spa, and Number Town.

5.   Use the list and another source, such as the newspaper want ads, to find all the different kinds of mechanics, computer workers, engineers, doctors, designers, artists, inspectors, managers, reporters, clerks, supervisors, technicians, and writers.

From *The Teacher's Book of Lists* © 1979, Goodyear Publishing Company, Inc.

TEAMS OF MAJOR U.S. SPORTS

Baseball

Atlanta Braves
Baltimore Orioles
Boston Red Sox
California Angels
Chicago Cubs
Chicago White Sox

Cincinnati Reds
Cleveland Indians
Detroit Tigers
Houston Astros
Kansas City Royals
Los Angeles Dodgers

Milwaukee Brewers
Minnesota Twins
Montreal Expos
New York Mets
New York Yankees
Oakland A's

Philadelphia Phillies
Pittsburgh Pirates
St. Louis Cardinals
San Diego Padres
San Francisco Giants
Texas Rangers

Basketball

Atlanta Hawks
Boston Celtics
Chicago Bulls
Cleveland Cavaliers
Denver Nuggets
Detroit Pistons

Golden State Warriors
Houston Rockets
Indiana Pacers
Kansas City Kings
Los Angeles Lakers
Milwaukee Bucks

New Jersey Nets
New Orleans Jazz
New York
   Knickerbockers
Philadelphia 76er's
Phoenix Suns

Portland Trailblazers
San Antonio Spurs
San Diego Clippers
Seattle SuperSonics
Washington Bullets

Football

Atlanta Falcons
Baltimore Colts
Buffalo Bills
Chicago Bears
Cincinnati Bengals
Cleveland Browns
Dallas Cowboys

Denver Broncos
Detroit Lions
Green Bay Packers
Houston Oilers
Kansas City Chiefs
Los Angeles Rams
Miami Dolphins

Minnesota Vikings
New England Patriots
New Orleans Saints
New York Giants
New York Jets
Oakland Raiders
Philadelphia Eagles

Pittsburgh Steelers
St. Louis Cardinals
San Diego Chargers
San Francisco 49er's
Seattle Seahawks
Tampa Bay Buccaneers
Washington Redskins

Hockey

Atlanta Flames
Birmingham Bulls
Boston Bruins
Buffalo Sabres
Calgary Cowboys
Chicago Black Hawks
Cincinnati Stingers
Cleveland Barons

Colorado Rockies
Detroit Red Wings
Edmonton Oilers
Houston Aeros
Indianapolis Racers
Los Angeles Kings
Minnesota Fighting
   Saints

Minnesota North Stars
Montreal Canadiens
New England Whalers
New York Islanders
New York Rangers
Philadelphia Flyers
Phoenix Roadrunners
Pittsburgh Penguins

Quebec Nordiques
St. Louis Blues
San Diego Mariners
Toronto Maple Leafs
Vancouver Canucks
Washington Capitals
Winnipeg Jets

MODERN OLYMPIC GAMES—DATES AND LOCATIONS

The first modern Olympics in 1896 had nine nations represented. Today more than one hundred nations send athletes to compete.

Summer Games	**Winter Games**
1896 Athens, Greece	
1900 Paris, France	
1904 St. Louis, Missouri, U.S.A.	
1906 Athens, Greece (unofficial)	
1908 London, England	
1912 Stockholm, Sweden	
1920 Antwerp, Belgium	
1924 Paris, France	1924 Chamonix, France
1928 Amsterdam, Netherlands	1928 St. Moritz, Switzerland
1932 Los Angeles, California, U.S.A.	1932 Lake Placid, New York, U.S.A.
1936 Berlin, Germany	1936 Garmisch-Partenkirchen, Germany
1948 London, England	1948 St. Moritz, Switzerland
1952 Helsinki, Finland	1952 Oslo, Norway
1956 Melbourne, Australia	1956 Cortina d'Ampezzo, Italy
1960 Rome, Italy	1960 Squaw Valley, California, U.S.A.
1964 Tokyo, Japan	1964 Innsbruck, Austria
1968 Mexico City, Mexico	1968 Grenoble, France
1972 Munich, Germany	1972 Sapporo, Japan
1976 Montreal, Canada	1976 Innsbruck, Austria
1980 Scheduled for Moscow, U.S.S.R.	1980 Scheduled for Lake Placid, New York, U.S.A.

ONESIES, TWOSIES—JACKS GAMES

These games were written for right-handers. The instructions can be reversed for left-handed players, and can be played through to "twosies," "threesies," etc.

Around the World

onesies: Throw the ball up and pick up a jack. Before catching the ball, circle the ball clockwise with your hand, ending underneath the ball to catch it. Put the jacks in your left hand.

Bouncing Babies

onesies: Throw the ball up with your left hand. Pick up a jack with your right hand, then catch the ball with your left hand. The ball must be caught after you pick up the jack.

Breaking Eggs ("Knocksies")

onesies: Throw the ball up, pick up a jack, knock it on the floor once, and put it in your left hand. Then catch the ball before it bounces more than once.

Flying Dutchman

onesies: Throw the ball up, pick up a jack, catch the ball in your right hand before it bounces more than once. Hold the ball back on your palm and the jack forward on your fingers and toss both into the air. Catch the jack in your left hand, let the ball bounce once before you catch it in your right hand.

Picking Cherries (Cherries in the Basket)

onesies: Throw the ball up, pick up a jack, and put it in your left hand (the basket). Then catch the ball in your right hand before it bounces more than once.

Pigs in the Pen

Form the pen by cupping your left hand and putting it down with the side of your little finger and the side of your thumb lying flat on the floor. The pen may not be moved until you have completed a series (onesies, twosies, etc.).

onesies: Throw the ball up and, with your right hand, slide one jack into the pen. Then catch the ball before it bounces more than once.

Sheep Over the Fence

Make the fence by placing the side of your left hand perpendicular to the floor. This fence may not be moved until you have completed a series (onesies, twosies, etc.).

onesies: Throw the ball up, pick up one jack, and put it on the other side of the "fence." Then catch the ball with your right hand before it bounces more than once.

Shooting Stars

onesies: Throw the ball up, pick up a jack, and catch the ball with your right hand before it bounces more than once. Hold the ball back on the palm of your hand with your thumb and leave the jack forward on your fingers. Toss the jack up about 6 inches in the air and catch it with your left hand.

Adapted from Marta Weigle, *Jacks and Jack Games: Follow My Fancy* (New York: Dover, 1970).

JUMP ROPE RHYMES

Add to the children's jump rope repertoire with these jump rope rhymes. Make use of them in another way by charting the rhymes and putting them on a Copycat Rack. Since many children like having their own copies, they will enjoy copying the rhymes for handwriting practice. Some other fun things to copy are recipes, song lyrics, and jokes.

Down by the ocean,
Down by the sea,
Johnny broke a milk bottle
And blamed it on me.
I told Ma and Ma told Pa,
Johnny got a lickin'
Ha! Ha! Ha!
How many lickin's did he get?
1, 2, 3, ...

John and Mary up in a tree,
K-I-S-S-I-N-G
First comes love,
Then comes marriage,
Here comes Mary
With a baby carriage.

I'm a little Dutch girl dressed in blue,
Here are the things I like to do:
Salute to the captain, bow to the queen,
Turn my back on the naughty, naughty king.
I can do the tap dance, I can do the split,
I can do the holka polka, just like this.
1, 2, 3, ...

Ice cream soda,
Delaware punch,
Tell me the initials
Of your honeybunch.
A, B, C, D, E . . . . . .

Cinderella dressed in yellow,
Went upstairs to see her fellow.
How many kisses did she get?
1, 2, 3, ...

Cinderella dressed in yellow,
Went upstairs to kiss her fellow.
By mistake, she kissed a snake.
How many doctors did it take?
1, 2, 3, ...

Anna Banana
Played the piana.
All she knew was the Star Spangled Banner.
She wiggles, she waggles,
And does the split,
And when she misses, she misses like this.

My mother, your mother, live across the way,
Three sixteen, East Broadway.
Every time they have a fight, this what they say:
Lady, lady turn around,
Lady, lady touch the ground,
Lady, lady show your shoes,
Lady, lady out goes YOU.

Policeman, policeman
Do your duty,
Here comes (name of person),
The American beauty.
She can do the rhumba,
She can do the splits,
She can wear her skirts
Up over her hips.

Teddy Bear, Teddy Bear, turn around,
Teddy Bear, Teddy Bear, touch the ground.
Teddy Bear, Teddy Bear, tie your shoes,
Teddy Bear, Teddy Bear, read the news.
Teddy Bear, Teddy Bear, go upstairs,
Teddy Bear, Teddy Bear, say your prayers.
Teddy Bear, Teddy Bear, turn out the light,
Teddy Bear, Teddy Bear, say goodnight.

Mother, Mother, I am ill,
Call for the doctor over the hill.
In comes the doctor,
In comes the nurse,
In comes the lady with the alligator purse.
"Mumps," said the doctor,
"Measles," said the nurse,
"Nothing," said the lady with the alligator
    purse.

The following jump rope rhymes were contributed by Janet Dubman's
fourth grade class, Centinela School, Inglewood, California.

Cinderella thinks she's cute,
All she wears is a bathing suit.
If she counts to twenty-one,
You may have another turn.
1, 2, 3, ...

Jugs, Jugs,
Mama's gonna have a baby,
It ain't no boy,
It ain't no girl,
It's just an ordinary baby.
Wrap it up in tissue paper,
Throw it down the elevator.
First floor, STOP. (stop rope)
Second floor, STOP. (stop rope)
Third floor, STOP. (stop rope)
'Cause here comes the baby with the H-O-T.

Blue bells, cockle shells,
Eevie, ivy, over.
Mama's in the kitchen cookin' rice,
Daddy's outside, shootin' dice.
Baby's in the cradle, fast asleep,
And here come sister with the H-O-T.

Late last night or the night before,
Twenty-four robbers came a-knockin' at
        my door,
I let one in,
He hit me on the head with a rolling pin,
I ran outside,
The other one came in,
I got so scared, I went to bed.

SENIOR CITIZENS—ANCIENT CIVILIZATIONS

Ancient Egyptian	c. 3100–30 B.C.
Assyrian	c. 1100–600 B.C.
Aztec	1300s–1519 A.D.
Babylonian	c. 2000–1100 B.C.
Etruscan	800–500 B.C. (height of power)
Harappa (Indus Valley)	2500–1500 B.C.
Hittites	2000–1000 B.C.
Incan	1450–1532 A.D. (height of power)
Khmer civilization (Cambodia)	800–1200 A.D. (height of power)
Mayan	200–900 A.D. (height of power)
Minoan	1700–1400? B.D. (height of power)
Mycenaean	1400–1100 B.C. (height of power on mainland Greece)
Sumerian	c. 3200–2000 B.C.

Questions on Ancient Civilizations

1. Where was the civilization located?
2. What geographical features favored the development of the civilization?
3. How were the remains discovered or excavated?
4. What is known about the buildings?
5. What are some of the unanswered questions about the civilization?
6. What are some of the artifacts and works of art that remain? What do they tell about the people?
7. How was the civilization ruled?
8. What were some of the religious practices of the civilization?
9. What are some unique contributions or developments of the civilization?
10. What were the causes of the decline of the civilization?
11. What was the economy of the civilization based on?
12. Did the civilization have slaves? Where were they from? How were they treated?
13. List the civilizations in chronological order.

From *The Teacher's Book of Lists* © 1979, Goodyear Publishing Company, Inc.

nine
ANIMALS

GOING, GOING, GONE
ENDANGERED AND EXTINCT ANIMALS

The endangered species on this list were obtained from the volumes of the *Red Data Book* compiled by the IUCN (International Union for the Conservation of Nature). Animals were selected to illustrate the various reasons for the decline of wildlife and the many kinds of species affected.

Going—classified as rare or vulnerable and likely to move into the endangered category in the near future if the reasons for their decline continue

Ceylon elephant found in eastern and southeastern Ceylon—killed by farmers whose lands are destroyed by migrating herds

Chimpanzee found in equatorial forests of Africa—captured for use in biomedical sciences as subjects for experiments, as pets, and for the animal trade; hunted for food and sport

Chinchilla found in Andes mountains of Chile and Bolivia—hunted and killed for its fur

Shortnose sturgeon, a small fish inhabiting Atlantic seaboard rivers—pollution of waters is a major factor as well as overfishing

Going—in danger of extinction; survival is not likely if the reasons for their decline continue

American crocodile found in Florida, Central America, parts of Mexico—killed for skins and sport; destruction of habitat, sometimes killed as a nuisance in docks

Arabian oryx found in Oman—they are declining because of uncontrolled hunting by organized hunting parties using cars and planes to overtake the animal

Beautiful parakeet found in Australia—main cause of extinction is excessive hunting and trapping for the aviculturist

Aye-Aye, forest-dwelling lemur of Madagascar—have suffered loss of habitat through forest clearance; killed by Malagasy people for superstitious reasons

Ciçek, a fish of Lake Egridir, Turkey—preyed upon by the pike-perch introduced in the lake in 1953, may already be extinct

Javan rhinoceros found in Indonesia—victims of overhunting for so-called medicinal products derived from their horns and blood

Orangutan, an ape inhabiting Borneo and Sumatra—destruction of forest habitat, captured for use by pet dealers, zoos, and research laboratories

Round Island boa found in Round Island (northwest of Mauritius)—goats and rabbits introduced to the island destroyed the ecological balance by eating the grasses leading to a reduction in the number of insects; insect-eating lizards used by the boa as food then diminished

San Francisco garter snake found in California—destruction of habitat due to housing development projects, control of waterflow, and removal of vegetation

South American river turtle (or arrau) found in tropical South America—hunted for eggs which are considered a delicacy, oil, meat, and the pet trade

Whooping crane, North America's tallest bird—victim of overhunting; loss of habitat due to drainage and fill of marshes

Gone—extinct

Arabian ostrich found in Saudi Arabia—hunted for sport in automobiles and airplanes

Catabasis acuminatus, a fish of the Rio Tieté, Brazil—pollution of headwaters of river by sewage from the city of São Paulo

Great auk found in Northern Europe and North America—killed for eggs, flesh, and feathered skin

Passenger pigeon found in eastern North America—trapped and shot for food and sport

Going, Going, Gone Activities

1. "Adopt" an endangered animal. Start a campaign to save it by writing pamphlets and slogans, making posters and bumper stickers.

2. On a world map, locate the country or countries where the endangered species are presently found. Make symbols to represent the animals' present status and place your symbols on the map.

3. Write fables or "Just So" stories to explain why an animal is endangered or extinct. Use factual information or make up your own. Here are some examples of titles: Bye-bye, Aye-aye; The Passing of the Passenger Pigeon; How the Chinchilla Lost Its Coat; The Ciçek and the Pike-Perch.

4. Make a list of *other endangered and extinct things.* Endangered things might include buildings or historic sites in your city, the circus, hula hoops, and the door-to-door milkman; 23¢ a gallon for gas, the 5¢ cigar, Indian-head pennies, and the Pony Express could be on the extinct list.

ROCK-A-BYE BABY—NAMES FOR ANIMAL OFFSPRING

Animal	Offspring	Animal	Offspring
bear	cub	kangaroo	joey
beaver	kit	lion	cub
cat	kitten	otter	whelp
chicken	chick	oyster	spat
cow	calf	pig	piglet, farrow, shoat
deer	fawn	rabbit	bunny
dog	pup, puppy	rhinoceros	calf
eagle	eaglet	seal	pup
eel	elver	sheep	lamb
elephant	calf	swan	cygnet
fox	cub, kit	tiger	cub
giraffe	calf	turkey	poult
goat	kid	whale	calf
goose	gosling	wolf	cub, whelp
hawk	eyas		
horse	foal		

HERDS, SCHOOLS, AND FLOCKS—NAMES FOR ANIMAL GROUPS

Animal	Group Name	Animal	Group Name
badgers	cete	goats	flock
bears	sloth	hawks	cast
beavers	colony	hogs	drift
bees	swarm	horses	herd
buffalo	gang	kangaroos	troop, mob
cats	clowder	lions	pride
chickens	flock	mallards	sord
chicks	clutch	monkeys	troop
cows	herd	partridges	covey
dogs	pack	peacocks	muster
ducks	brace, flock	pheasants	nide
elephants	herd	pigs	drove, litter
elks	gang	quails	bevy
fish	school	rabbits	colony
foxes	skulk	seals	pod
geese	flock, gaggle (usually when grouped together on water)	sheep	drove, flock
		turkeys	rafter
		whales	gam, pod
		wolves	pack, rout

6'S AND 8'S
PICTURESQUE NAMES OF INSECTS AND SPIDERS

ant lion
assassin bug
back swimmer
bald-faced hornet
bedbug
beefly
big green darner dragonfly
black widow spider
blister beetle
buffalo tree hopper
burying beetle
cabbage butterfly
carpenter ant
carpenter bee
carpet beetle
confused flower beetle
corn earworm
daddy longlegs (harvestman)
deathwatch beetle
dog-faced butterfly
earwig
engraver beetle

firefly
garden springtail
goliath beetle
greenbottle fly
gypsy moth
harlequin bug
June bug
lacewing
lady beetle (lady bug)
lightning bug
longhorn beetle
mayfly
monarch butterfly
paper wasp
praying mantis
punkies, no-see-ums (fly)
red admiral butterfly
robber fly
scorpion fly
silverfish
snowy tree cricket
soldier beetle

squashbug
squint-eye spider
sphinx moth
striped cucumber beetle
swallowtail butterfly
tarnished plant bug
tiger moth
tortoise beetle
trapdoor spider
triangle spider
turret spider
two-striped grasshopper
wanderer butterfly
water boatman
water penny beetle
water strider
whirligig beetle
wolf spider
yellow jacket
yellow woolybear (moth)
zebra spider

Activities With Insects and Spiders

1. Draw several of the insects and spiders as you think they would look, according to their names. Then compare your drawings with pictures of how the insects and spiders really look.

2. Categorize the insects and spiders into helpful and harmful groups.

3. Categorize the insects and spiders by their names, into groups such as colors, foods, animals, and jobs.

From *The Teacher's Book of Lists* © 1979, Goodyear Publishing Company, Inc.

FAMOUS ANIMAL PEOPLE

Louis Agassiz—U.S. naturalist; famed for work on living and fossil forms of fish

J. J. Audubon—famous American naturalist and artist; one of the first to study and paint U.S. birds

Spencer F. Baird—naturalist and vertebrate zoologist

Rachel Carson—American marine biologist and science writer

Frank Chapman—American ornithologist; one of the first to study birds with the camera

Baron Cuvier—French naturalist; first to compare the structure of animal bodies with that of man

Charles Darwin—British naturalist; developed theory of evolution based on natural selection that revolutionized the biological sciences

Raymond Lee Ditmars—noted American authority on reptiles; wrote many popular reptile books; developed a snakebite serum

William Henry Hudson—English author and naturalist; wrote articles and books on nature, particularly bird life

Sir Julian Huxley—noted British biologist

Thomas Huxley—famous zoologist, lecturer, and writer

Carolus Linnaeus—developed a scientific classification system of animals and plants

Clinton Hart Merriam—American physician and zoologist; helped found the National Geographic Society in 1888

Jan Swammerdam—Dutch anatomist and zoologist; pioneered in the anatomy of insects; his work formed the basis of entomology

Nicolaas Tinbergen—Dutch-born zoologist; studies how behavior of animals adapts to the environment

Jane Goodall Van Lawick—English zoologist; became famous for behavior studies of chimpanzees

Alexander Wilson—one of the founders of American ornithology

From The Teacher's Book of Lists © 1979, Goodyear Publishing Company, Inc.

ANIMALOGISTS

biologist—scientist who studies living organisms

biosociologist—an ecologist who studies environments of groups of living things, such as schools of fish

conchologist—zoologist who studies mollusks or shells

ecologist—biologist who studies the relationship between organisms and their environment

embryologist—biologist who studies the formation and development of living things prior to birth

entomologist—zoologist who specializes in the study of insects

helminthologist—zoologist who studies worms

herpetologist—zoologist who studies reptiles and amphibians

ichthyologist—zoologist who specializes in the study of fishes

limnologist—biologist who studies the biological, chemical, geographical, and physical features of lakes and ponds (fresh waters)

malacologist—zoologist who studies mollusks

mammalogist—zoologist who specializes in the study of mammals

morphologist—biologist who examines animal form and structure

ornithologist—zoologist who specializes in the study of birds

physiologist—biologist who studies the normal functions of living things

taxonomist—scientist who names and classifies animals

zoographer—an ecologist who studies the distribution of animals in the various regions of the world

zoologist—scientist who studies animals and their classification

AWARDS TO ANIMALS

Selecting an animal to study can be more fun if you know some interesting animal facts. Here are some animals who have earned awards for outstanding achievement. These awards can be displayed in an *awards gallery* from which children choose an animal to study.

Maxi Awards

blue whale—largest and heaviest mammal

African elephant—largest land animal

giraffe—tallest animal

Kodiak bear—largest land carnivore

Siberian tiger—largest member of the cat family

springboks—largest herds

gorilla—largest primate

mandrill—largest member of the monkey family

Irish wolfhound—tallest breed of dog

ostrich—largest bird, with the largest eye of any land animal

giant squid—largest eye of any living or extinct animal, land or sea

wandering albatross—bird with the largest wing span

bald eagle—builds the largest nests

crocodile—largest reptile

Komodo monitor—largest lizard

anaconda—longest and heaviest of all snakes

Chinese giant salamander—largest amphibian

goliath frog—largest frog

marine toad—largest toad

whale shark—largest fish

white shark—largest carnivorous fish

nephila spider—has the largest spider web

goliath beetle—heaviest insect

stick-insect—longest insect

giant birdwing—largest butterfly*

*Most probable.

Mini Awards

pygmy shrew—smallest mammal

sea otter—smallest totally marine mammal

bee hummingbird—smallest bird

gecko—smallest reptile*

thread snake—shortest snake*

dwarf pygmy goby—shortest fish*

common housefly—shortest-lived insect*

dwarf blue butterfly—smallest butterfly*

*Most probable.

From *The Guinness Book of Animal Facts and Feats,* Gerald L. Wood (Guinness Superlatives Ltd., Great Britain, 1972)

From *The Teacher's Book of Lists* © 1979, Goodyear Publishing Company, Inc.

Tortoise and Hare Awards

pronghorn antelope—fastest land animal over a sustained distance

cheetah—fastest land animal over a short distance

three-toed sloth—slowest moving land mammal

spine-tailed swift—fastest flying bird

black mamba—fastest moving land snake*

dragonfly—fastest flying insect

marlin—fastest fish over a sustained distance

sea horse—slowest moving marine fish

Senior Citizens Award

killer whale—longest-lived mammal (except man)

Asiatic elephant—longest-lived land mammal (except man)

queen termite—longest-lived insect

Bad Guy Awards

king cobra—longest venomous snake

diamondback rattler—heaviest venomous snake

Kokoi arrow poison frog—most poisonous animal ever recorded

Maternity Award

Asiatic elephant—longest mammal gestation period

The Now Hear This Award

bat—most highly developed sense of hearing (among mammals)

Broad Jump Award

red kangaroo—longest recorded leap

Bon Voyage Award

Arctic tern—longest migration of flying birds

Whiz Kids Award

chimpanzee—most intelligent primate (except man)

baboon—most intelligent member of the monkey family

stonefish—most venomous sting

Japanese puffer fish—most poisonous fish if eaten

piranha—most ferocious fish

black widow—most venomous spider

blue-ringed octopus—most dangerous octopus

The Big Sleep Award

edible dormouse—mammal longest in hibernation

Thick Skin Award

whale shark—the thickest skin of any animal

Loud Mouth Award

male cicada—loudest insect

Architect's Award

termites—master builders of the world

*Most probable.

Beastly Questions

1. Why could the ziczac be called "the crocodile's best friend"?
2. Where would you find some pinnipeds?
3. Which animal would get the Most Unusual Animal Award? Why?
4. Why do some animals estivate?
5. Why are some people called "dodos"?
6. What do the aardvark and the anteater have in common?
7. What is the bear's "Keep-Out" sign?
8. In the old days, why did women who wore corsets need whales?
9. How does a zoo rhino or elephant get a pedicure?
10. How does the platypus break all the rules of nature?
11. Why can't ants be called "litterbugs"?
12. How does the cave fish manage without any eyes?
13. How would you prepare for a hermit crab houseguest?
14. What five features makes the camel well adapted for desert travel?
15. What do the cows, horses, and dogs of the ocean look like?
16. How do you feed a giraffe?
17. What are some special jobs dogs are trained to do?
18. What are an *Adobenus rosmarus* and a *Thalarctos maritimus*?
19. What would you find in a Tiergarten?
20. What is a pangolin?
21. How is a jerboa like a kangaroo?
22. Which animals ruminate?
23. How do birds sing?
24. How does a raccoon carry its babies?
25. How does a flying squirrel fly?
26. Why don't spiders get caught in their own webs?
27. What does the S.P.C.A. do for animals?
28. How does a bat "see with its ears"?
29. What's odd about the way sloths live?
30. What is the layout of a prairie dog's home?
31. Where does a snake's tail begin?
32. What does a lepidopterist collect?
33. What happens when insects stridulate?
34. Why can a fly walk on the ceiling?
35. How are an octopus and a squid like a jet?

From *The Teacher's Book of Lists* © 1979, Goodyear Publishing Company, Inc.

THE _____ AWARD

IS PRESENTED TO _____
                    animal's name

FOR _____
     (animal's outstanding characteristic)

Description of Animal: _____
Habitat: _____
Interesting Facts: _____
_____

Draw a picture of the animal in its natural habitat and paste in here.

Name:
Date:

DINOSAURS

ALLOSAURUS meat eater

more than thirty feet long

moved on two large hind legs, used powerful tail for support in walking or standing

ANATOSAURUS plant eater

about forty feet long

walked on two legs, used tail for support; had as many as 2,000 teeth

ANKYLOSAURUS plant eater

about ten feet long

body was covered with overlapping bony plates with a row of spikes along each side; clublike tail tipped with a heavy mass of bone

BRACHIOSAURUS   plant eater

seventy feet long,
weighed eighty-four
short tons

largest of all the
dinosaurs

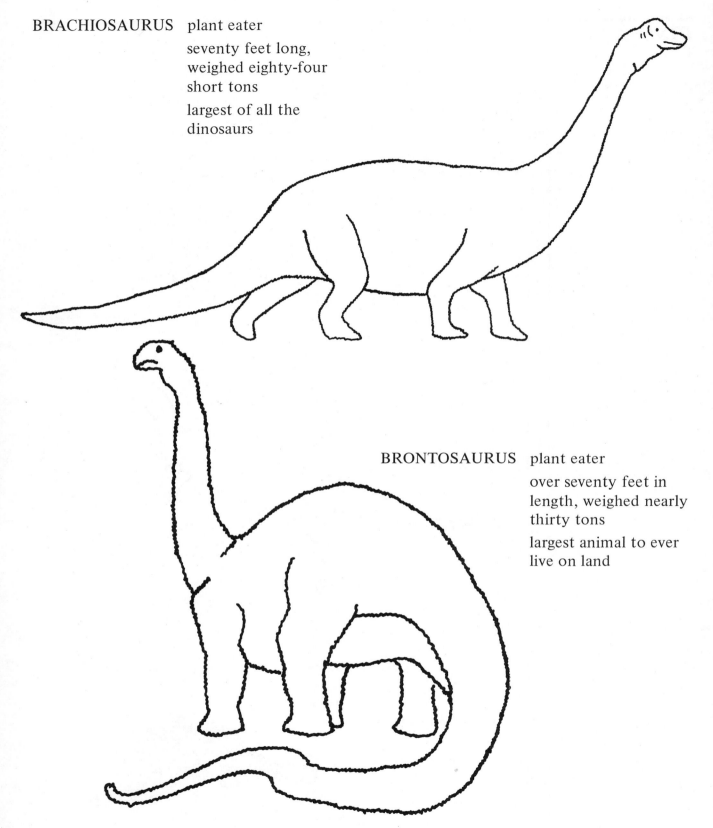

BRONTOSAURUS   plant eater

over seventy feet in
length, weighed nearly
thirty tons

largest animal to ever
live on land

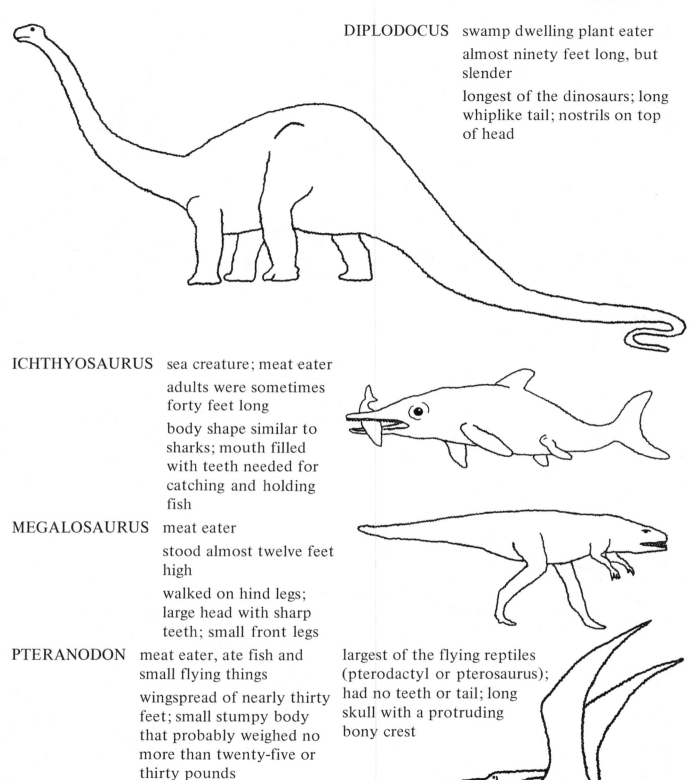

DIPLODOCUS swamp dwelling plant eater

almost ninety feet long, but slender

longest of the dinosaurs; long whiplike tail; nostrils on top of head

ICHTHYOSAURUS sea creature; meat eater

adults were sometimes forty feet long

body shape similar to sharks; mouth filled with teeth needed for catching and holding fish

MEGALOSAURUS meat eater

stood almost twelve feet high

walked on hind legs; large head with sharp teeth; small front legs

PTERANODON meat eater, ate fish and small flying things

wingspread of nearly thirty feet; small stumpy body that probably weighed no more than twenty-five or thirty pounds

largest of the flying reptiles (pterodactyl or pterosaurus); had no teeth or tail; long skull with a protruding bony crest

STEGOSAURUS plant eater

about eighteen feet long

triangular bony plates
protected its neck, back,
and tail; brain about the
size of a walnut

TRACHODON plant eater

thirty to forty feet long

duck-billed; walked on hind
legs

TRICERATOPS plant eater

twenty-five feet long

bony armor covered head;
three horns protruded from
head

TYRANNOSAURUS REX largest meat eater

measured fifty feet from nose to tail, stood about twenty feet high

had six-inch razor-sharp teeth

Dinosaur Activities

1. Make a graph of the lengths of the dinosaurs.
2. Categorize the dinosaurs into two groups, carnivores and herbivores.
3. Convert the lengths of the dinosaurs into meters.
4. Use the length of a car, bed, or other large thing as a unit of measure. Convert the lengths of the dinosaurs into this unit. For example, ankylosaurus = about one car
5. Choose a dinosaur and a familiar melody. Make up lyrics to fit the melody, using the information on the dinosaur list. Here's a song about a trachodon to be sung to the melody of Three Blind Mice.

Trachodon, Trachodon,

Duck-billed mouth, duck-billed mouth,

He walked about on his two hind legs,

His length was thirty to forty feet,

Did you ever see such a sight in your life as Trachodon.

THE ARTS

ten
ART AND MUSIC

HUES, BLUES, AND FUGUES
ART AND MUSIC CATEGORIES

Here's a list of art and music pieces grouped within some interesting categories. One way to use this list is to integrate a category with a usual topic of study. For example, Wind, Rain, Sleet, and Snow can be combined with a study of weather or the seasons. Another way is to begin with a category and expand into other subject areas and skills. For example, art and music activities that take place as a result of exposure to works in the category, Beauty in the Beast, can lead to other experiences. These experiences might include writing original stories and poems, reading animal tales, and making scientific reports and observations.

Art

SHOW BIZ

Le Cirque—Georges Seurat

La Parade (The Side Show)—Georges Seurat

Broadway Boogie Woogie—Piet Mondrian

Three Musicians—Pablo Picasso

Three Dancers—Pablo Picasso

Clown—Henri de Toulouse-Lautrec

Cafe Concert at Les Ambassadeurs—Edgar Degas

Rehearsal in the Foyer of the Opera—Edgar Degas

Music

SHOW BIZ

Circus Polka—Igor Stravinsky

"The Shrovetide Fair" from Petrouchka Ballet Suite—Igor Stravinsky

"Vesti La Giubba" from Pagliacci—Ruggiero Leoncavallo

"Clowns" from A Midsummer Night's Dream—Felix Mendelssohn

"Circus Music" from The Red Pony—Aaron Copland

Art
COLORS

Composition in Red, Blue, and Yellow—
Piet Mondrian

Harmony in Red—Henri Matisse

Park Near L(ucerne)—Paul Klee

The Red Studio—Henri Matisse

Cow's Skull—Red, White, and Blue—
Georgia O'Keeffe

ON THE ROAD

End of the Trail—James Earle Fraser

In the Catskills—Thomas Cole

View of Toledo—El Greco
(Domenicos Theotocopoulos)

The Scout: Friends or Enemies?
—Frederick Remington

Boulevard Montmartre, Paris
—Camille Pissarro

ALL IN THE FAMILY

The Family—Marisol

Arrangement in Black and Grey:
The Artist's Mother—James McNeill
Whistler

An Old Man and His Grandson
—Domenico Ghirlandaio

The Peale Family—Charles Willson Peale

Mother and Child with Bird
—Suzuki Harunobu

American Gothic—Grant Wood

The Mother and Sister of the Artist
—Berthe Morisot

A Father's Curse: The Ungrateful Son
—Jean Baptiste Greuze

Family Promenade—Paul Klee

Music
COLORS

Rhapsody in Blue—George Gershwin

Fantasia on "Greensleeves"—English folk
song, composer unknown—adapted and
orchestrated by Ralph Vaughn Williams

Mood Indigo—Duke Ellington

Le Train bleu—Darius Milhaud

Ebony Concerto—Igor Stravinsky

ON THE ROAD

An American in Paris—George Gershwin

Grand Canyon Suite—Ferde Grofé

The Little Train of Caipira
—Heitor Villa-Lobos

St. Louis Blues—W. C. Handy

Cockaigne (In London Town)
—Sir Edward Elgar

In the Steppes of Central Asia
—Alexander Borodin

ALL IN THE FAMILY

The Cradle Song—Johannes Brahms

"Brother Come and Dance with Me" from
Hansel and Gretel—Engelbert Humperdinck

The Nursery—Modest Moussorgsky

The Bartered Bride—Bedřich Smetana

"The Bridal Procession" from Lohengrin
—Richard Wagner

Prole do Bébé (Baby's Family)
—Heitor Villa-Lobos

"Curious Story" from Kinderscenen
—Robert Schumann

Art
A.M. AND P.M.

The Starry Night—Vincent Van Gogh

An Impression: Sunrise—Claude Monet

Nighthawks—Edward Hopper

Day and Night—M. C. Escher

WHAT'S MY LINE?

The Gleaners—Jean François Millet

The Sower—Jean François Millet

The Lacemaker—Jan Vermeer

Washerwomen—Honoré Daumier

The Stone Breakers—Gustave Courbet

Sugar Cane—Diego Rivera

Wagon Boss—Charles Russell

The Anatomy Lesson—Rembrandt van Rijn

Jockeys in the Rain—Edgar Degas

The Boxers—Alexander Archipenko

H_2O

Hollow of the Deep-Sea Wave —Katsushika Hokusai

Water Lillies—Claude Monet

The Boating Party—Mary Cassatt

Breezing Up—Winslow Homer

Fur Traders on the Missouri—George Caleb Bingham

Wave, Night—Georgia O'Keeffe

Music
A.M. AND P.M.

Vincent (Starry, Starry Night)—Don McLean

Moonlight Sonata—Ludwig van Beethoven

Morning Mood from "Peer Gynt" —Edvard Grieg

Nights in the Gardens of Spain —Manuel de Falla

Stardust—Hoagy Carmichael

WHAT'S MY LINE?

The Barber of Seville—Gioacchino Rossini

Sorcerer's Apprentice—Paul Dukas

Rodeo—Aaron Copland

Spinning Song—Franz Schubert

Spinning Song, Op. 67, No. 4—Felix Mendelssohn

"Where Are the Clowns?" from A Little Night Music—Stephen Sondheim

H.M.S. Pinafore—Gilbert and Sullivan

Zar und Zimmermann (The Czar and the Carpenter)—Albert Lortzing

The Harmonius Blacksmith—George Frederick Handel

H_2O

La Mer—Claude Debussy

"Barcarolle" from The Tales of Hoffmann —Jacques Offenbach

Venetian Boat Song—Felix Mendelssohn

Die Moldau—Bedřich Smetana

On the Beautiful Blue Danube—Johann Strauss

"The Rhine Motive" from Das Rheingeld —Richard Wagner

Water Music—George Frederick Handel

Art
THE ARTS IN ART

High Kick—Edgar Degas

The Yellow Violin—Raoul Dufy

Musical Forms—Georges Braque

The Artist in His Studio—Jan Vermeer

Claude Monet in His Floating Studio
—Èdouard Manet

MOTHER NATURE

Flowering Trees—Piet Mondrian

Blue Landscape—Paul Cézanne

Hampstead Heath—John Constable

May Day—Andrew Wyeth

Photographs by Eliot Porter and
Ansel Adams

DREAMS AND FANTASY

The Dream—Henri Rousseau

Sweet Dreams—Paul Gauguin

The Harlequin's Carnival—Joan Miró

Casa Milá Apartment House, Barcelona
—Antoni Gaudí

Church of Notre-Dame-du-Haut
—Le Corbusier

I and the Village—Marc Chagall

Music
THE ARTS IN ART

Pictures from an Exhibition—Modest
Moussorgsky

Matthias the Painter—Paul Hindemith

Walt Whitman—Dmitri Shostakovich

Seven Studies on Themes of Paul Klee
—Gunther Schuller

"The Poet Speaks" from Kinderscenen
—Robert Schumann

MOTHER NATURE

Tales from the Vienna Woods
—Johann Strauss

Symphony No. 6 (The Pastoral)
—Ludwig van Beethoven

Out of Doors Suite—Béla Bártok

Spring Symphony—Robert Schumann

Italian Symphony—Felix Mendelssohn

My Country—Bedřich Smetana

"Waltz of the Flowers" from the
Nutcracker Suite—Peter Ilyich
Tchaikovsky

DREAMS AND FANTASY

Mother Goose Suite—Maurice Ravel

Hansel and Gretel—Engelbert Humperdinck

The Nutcracker Suite—Peter Ilyich
Tchaikovsky

Incidental Music to A Midsummer Night's
Dream—Felix Mendelssohn

Scheherazade—Nicholas Rimsky-Korsakoff

"The Fantasy Overture" from Romeo and
Juliet—Peter Ilyich Tchaikovsky

Firebird Suite—Igor Stravinsky

Art
NIGHTMARES
The Nightmare—John Henry Fuseli

The Dream—Max Beckmann

The Persistence of Memory—Salvador Dali

House of Stairs—M. C. Escher

The Garden of Delights—Hieronymus Bosch

The Storm—Yves Tanguy

The Scream—Edvard Munch

Demon as Pirate—Paul Klee

Swamp Angel—Max Ernst

BEAUTY IN THE BEAST
Two Bison—Lascaux cave painting

Crane—Katsushika Hokusai

Fantastic Rhinoceros—Albrecht Dürer

The Hare—Albrecht Dürer

Exotic Landscape—Henri Rousseau

Tiger in the Rain—Henri Rousseau

Peaceable Kingdom—Edward Hicks

Wild Turkey—J. J. Audubon

Bird in Space (sculpture)—Constantin Brancusi

Lobster Trap and Fish Tail (mobile)—Alexander Calder

Dog—Alberto Giacometti

THREE'S A CROWD
Peasant Dance—Pieter Bruegel

People Waiting—Honoré Daumier

The Night Watch—Rembrandt van Rijn

The School of Athens—Raphael

Visit of the Magi—Benozzo Gozzoli

Music
NIGHTMARES
Danse Macabre—Camille Saint-Saëns

Night on Bald Mountain—Modest Moussorgsky

Baba Yaga—Anatol Liadov

El Amor Brujo—Manuel de Falla

BEAUTY IN THE BEAST
Papillon No. 8—Robert Schumann

Papillon—Edvard Grieg

Flight of the Bumblebee—Nicholas Rimsky-Korsakoff

The Nightingale—Dmitri Shostakovich

The Swan Lake Ballet—Peter Ilyich Tchaikovsky

Afternoon of a Faun—Claude Debussy

Peter and the Wolf—Sergei Prokofiev

Carnival of the Animals—Camille Saint-Saëns

Bear Dance—Béla Bártok

THREE'S A CROWD
"Pilgrim's Chorus" from Tannhäuser—Richard Wagner

"Hallelujah Chorus" from Messiah—George Frederick Handel

Symphony No. 8, in Eb major (Symphony of a Thousand)—Gustav Mahler

From *The Teacher's Book of Lists* © 1979, Goodyear Publishing Company, Inc.

Art
GIVE ME YOUR TIRED, YOUR POOR . . .

The Third Class Carriage—Honoré Daumier

The Potato-Eaters—Vincent Van Gogh

Victims (detail from University of Guadalajara Mural Cycle)—José Clemente Orozco

Peasants Carrying Brushwood—Jean François Millet

The Liberation of the Peon—Diego Rivera

Breadline—Reginald Marsh

FUN AND GAMES

A Sunday Afternoon on the Grand Jatte—Georges Seurat

Swimmers—Katsushika Hokusai

Children's Games—Pieter Bruegel

Le Moulin de la Galette—Auguste Renoir

Bathers—Georges Seurat

The Card Players—Paul Cézanne

Boating—Èdouard Manet

Jockeys Before the Grandstand—Edgar Degas

WINING AND DINING

Campbell's Soup—Andy Warhol

The Basket of Apples—Paul Cézanne

Still Life—Diego Velázquez

Pie—Roy Lichtenstein

The Diner—George Segal

Giant Hamburger (sculpture)—Claes Oldenburg

Music
GIVE ME YOUR TIRED, YOUR POOR . . .

Porgy and Bess—George Gershwin

Peasant Cantata—Johann Sebastian Bach

La Bohème—Giacomo Puccini

Poet and Peasant Overture—Franz von Suppé

The Threepenny Opera—Kurt Weill, Bertholt Brecht

The Cradle Will Rock—Marc Blitzstein

Scenes from Peasant Life—Edvard Grieg

FUN AND GAMES

"The Toreador Song" from Carmen—Georges Bizet

Children's Games—Georges Bizet

Toy Symphony—Joseph Haydn

Till Eulenspiegel's Merry Pranks—Richard Strauss

Roman Carnival Overture—Louis Hector Berlioz

Camptown Races—Stephen Foster

WINING AND DINING

The Love for Three Oranges—Sergei Prokofiev

"Breakfast Waltz, Waiter's Waltz, Dinner Music" from Der Rosenkavalier—Richard Strauss

Yorkshire Feast Song—Henry Purcell

"The Drinking Song" from La Traviata—Giuseppe Verdi

Whipped Cream (ballet)—Richard Strauss

The Long Christmas Dinner—Paul Hindemith

Art

A HOUSE IS NOT A HOME

Taj Mahal, India

Mosque of Ahmed I, Istanbul

Notre-Dame, Paris

Pyramids, Egypt

Robie House, Chicago—Frank Lloyd Wright

Lake Shore Drive Apartment Houses —Mies Van der Rohe

Monticello—Thomas Jefferson

Parthenon, Athens

Kinkakuji (the Golden Pavilion), Kyoto

WIND, RAIN, SLEET, AND SNOW

Primavera—Sandro Botticelli

The Return of the Hunters—Pieter Bruegel

The Old Checkered House—Grandma Moses (Anna Mary Robertson Moses)

Waterloo Bridge (Effects of Mist) —Claude Monet

Landscapes of the Four Seasons —Tsunenobu

Threatening Weather—Rene Magritte

NUTS AND BOLTS

Computer Landscape—David Pease

Twittering Machine—Paul Klee

Brooklyn Bridge—Joseph Stella

Music

A HOUSE IS NOT A HOME

Skyscrapers (ballet)—John Alden Carpenter

My Old Kentucky Home—Stephen Foster

We Are Building a City (children's opera) —Paul Hindemith

Quiet City—Aaron Copland

WIND, RAIN, SLEET, AND SNOW

The Four Seasons—Antonio Vivaldi

Clouds, Mists—Claude Debussy

The Rite of Spring—Igor Stravinsky

"The Snow Is Dancing" from Children's Corner Suite—Claude Debussy

"The Storm and the Calm" from William Tell Overture—Gioacchino Rossini

Appalachian Spring—Aaron Copland

Summer Music for Woodwind Quartet —Samuel Barber

"A Masque of the Seasons" from The Fairy Queen—Henry Purcell

Raindrop Prelude—Frédéric Chopin

NUTS AND BOLTS

The Telephone—Gian-Carlo Menotti

Dance of Steel—Sergei Prokofiev

Catalogue of Agricultural Implements —Darius Milhaud

Pacific 231—Arthur Honneger

Art
WAR AND PEACE

Guernica—Pablo Picasso

The Executions of the 3rd of May
—Francisco de Goya

Battle of the Amazons
—Peter Paul Rubens

St. George—Donatello (sculpture)

Mona Lisa—Leonardo da Vinci

Recumbent Figure—Henry Moore
(sculpture)

Peace—Jacques Lipchitz (sculpture)

The Kiss—Auguste Rodin (sculpture)

The Kiss—Constantin Brancusi (sculpture)

Love—Robert Indiana (sculpture)

THIS IS ME

SELF-PORTRAITS

Leonardo da Vinci

Peter Paul Rubens

Rembrandt van Rijn

Henri Rousseau

Joan Miró

Amedeo Modigliani

Vincent Van Gogh

·Francisco de Goya

Hieronymus Bosch

HIDDEN PICTURES

The Adoration of the Magi
—Sandro Botticelli

The Maids of Honor—Diego
Velazquez

The Last Judgment—Michaelangelo

At the Moulin Rouge—Henri de
Toulouse-Lautrec

The Artist's Studio—Gustave Courbet

Music
WAR AND PEACE

March Militaire—Franz Schubert

Liebestraum—Franz Liszt

The Story of a Soldier—Igor Stravinsky

Light Cavalry Overture—von Suppe

1812 Overture—Peter Ilyich Tchaikovsky

Peace Train—Cat Stevens

Wellington's Victory or the Battle of
Vittoria—Ludwig van Beethoven

Peace—Cándido Portinari

THIS IS ME

SELF-PORTRAITS

From My Life—Bedřich Smetana

From Memories of Childhood
—Modest Moussorgsky

ART PERIODS AND STYLES

The following brief descriptions contain some of the significant characteristics of an art period or style. Although art experts sometimes disagree on exact dates and artists of a period or style, approximate dates and representative works that are generally agreed upon are listed.

Gothic (c. 1150 – 1500)

Originated in France in the mid 1100s and spread to England, Germany, Italy, and other parts of Europe during the 1200s; great heights, lightness, and grace characterized Gothic architecture; pointed arches and tall, slender columns rose to cross-ribbed vaulting supported by flying buttresses, and stained glass windows depicted religious stories. During this period many painters worked as illuminators, illustrating and decorating expensive manuscript copies of the Gospels and prayer books; compositions became richer and more complex; people were given distinguishing features and personalities, and greater attention was paid to detail of plants, trees, and flowers—species became recognizable; introduction of the third dimension as painters attempted to depict depth; other forms of Gothic art include stone carvings, iron screens, metalwork using filigree, enamels and precious stones, and tapestries.

Rheims Cathedral—France
Notre-Dame Cathedral—France
Chartres Cathedral—France
Westminster Abbey—England
Milan Cathedral—Italy
Giotto—Madonna Enthroned
Gentile da Fabriano—The Adoration of the Magi
Master Honoré—Prayer Book of Phillip the Fair

Renaissance (c. 1400 – 1600)

A characteristic of Renaissance art was the development of linear perspective in pictures, use of lights and shadows to create depth, and graceful figures with more attention paid to anatomy and realism.

Donatello—David
Fra Angelico—The Annunciation
Sandro Botticelli—The Birth of Venus
Titian—Bacchanal
Leonardo da Vinci—Mona Lisa
Raphael—School of Athens

Michelangelo—Moses
Jan van Eyck—The Arnolfini Wedding
Pieter Bruegel—Peasant Wedding
Albrecht Dürer—Knight, Death, and Devil

Mannerism (c. 1520 – 1600)

A term that defines the transitional period from the high Renaissance to Baroque; the art often portrayed a historic event as a contemporary happening; paintings were characterized by exaggerated poses and elongation of the human figure, strange perspective, and unsteady light.

Parmigianino—The Madonna with the Long Neck
Tintoretto—The Last Supper
El Greco—The Burial of Count Orgaz

Baroque (c. 1600 – 1750)

Baroque art and architecture is characterized by flowing movement, swelling forms, grandiose dimensions, great activity, and dramatic detail. Architecture, sculpture, and painting were frequently combined into an integral work of art; architects combined Classical and Renaissance elements such as columns, arches, and capitals; sweeping curves replaced rectangular areas; greater emphasis was placed on city planning and landscape design; artists used techniques such as foreshortening and asymmetrical designs; drama was heightened by the theatrical use of lighting.

Gian Lorenzo Bernini—Fountain of the Four Rivers, Piazza Navona, Rome
Francesco Borromini—S. Carl alle Quartro Fontane
Dominikus Zimmermann—Die Wies, Bavaria, Germany
Annibale Carracci—Farnese Gallery ceiling
Michelangelo Caravaggio—Calling of St. Matthew
Peter Paul Rubens—The Garden of Love
Diego Velazquez—The Maids of Honor
Frans Hals—Yonker Ramp and His Sweetheart
Rembrandt—Night Watch

Rococo (c. 1720 – 1780)

Style developed out of Baroque; art communicated a feeling of relaxation and gaiety as opposed to the serious, heroic style of Baroque; paintings characterized by bright, shimmering surfaces and poetic, light-hearted imaginary themes.

Jean Honoré Fragonard—The Swing
Antoine Watteau—Mezzetin

Neoclassicism (c. 1750 – 1850)

Evolved as a reaction against Baroque and Rococo; art and architecture is marked by simplicity of design and restraint in the use of ornamentation; paintings characterized by strong contrasts of color, firmly modeled forms, balance and order.

From *The Teacher's Book of Lists* © 1979, Goodyear Publishing Company, Inc.

Jean Auguste Dominique Ingres—Odalisque
Jacques Louis David—Napoleon Crossing the Alps

Romanticism (c. 1800 – 1840)

Paintings expressed the emotion and imagination of the artists; emotional and symbolic qualities of a myth often combined with the representation of an ordinary event or scene to create a feeling of mystery; paintings characterized by vigorous brush strokes, vibrant color and deep shadows.

Theodore Gericault—Mounted Officer of the Imperial Guard
Eugène Delacroix—Greece on the Ruins of Missolonghi
Honoré Daumier—The Third Class Carriage
Joseph M. W. Turner—The Slave Ship

Realism (c. 1848 – 1900)

Differed from Romanticism in its insistence upon fact without idealization, on the real rather than the imaginary or ideal, on the present rather than the past; paintings were based on the artist's unsentimental view of life around him; many European and American artists continue to paint in this style today.

Gustave Courbet—The Stone Breakers

Impressionism (c. 1870 – 1910)

Like the Realists, the Impressionists painted scenes of everyday life, but their painting style was based on the continual changes of nature—light transforming objects, reflections altering color and form. Painters reproduced the effect or "impression" of things at a particular moment in time, recorded what they saw rather than what they knew about an object. Favorite subjects included scenes from the world of entertainment—cafés, concerts, the theater; pictures characterized by gaiety, sparkle, shimmering, luminous colors, freshness of color, free brushwork.

Claude Monet—The Cathedral at Rouen
Edgar Degas—Woman with Chrysanthemums
Pierre Auguste Renoir—Lunch of the Boating Party at Bougival
Mary Cassatt—The Bath
Camille Pissarro—Afternoon at the Boulevard des Italiens

From *The Teacher's Book of Lists* © 1979, Goodyear Publishing Company, Inc.

Post Impressionism (c. 1886 – 1905)

Post Impressionists label a group of artists who had at first accepted Impressionism, but went beyond it in various directions; artists of this period were not bound by a common goal or style, but pursued individual styles.

Georges Seurat—La Baignade
Vincent van Gogh—Sunflowers
Paul Cézanne—Mont Sainte Victoire
Paul Gauguin—La Orana Maria

Expressionism (early 1900s)

Interpreted reality in a highly personal manner; paintings are often characterized by distortion and exaggeration of color and form.

Henri de Toulouse-Lautrec—Dance at the Moulin Rouge
Henri Rousseau—The Sleeping Gypsy

Fauvism (c. 1903 – 1907)

Labeled the *fauves* (wild beasts) when they shocked the public with paintings filled with brilliant colors, bold distortions, and simple designs; influenced and encouraged by non-European cultures to seek new ways to communicate emotions; paintings characterized by rich surface texture, lively pattern, discordant color combinations, and sweeping brushstrokes; expression of emotion was more important than objective representation; continued the trends begun by Van Gogh and Gauguin.

Henri Matisse—The Joy of Life
Georges Rouault—The Old King
Chaim Soutine—The Dead Fowl

Die Brucke (c. 1904 – 1913)

The name means the Bridge. Members of this German society produced paintings especially expressive of intense human feelings; used vigorous brushwork, bold lines, strong colors, and distorted contours.

Max Beckmann—The Dream
Emil Nolde—Masks and Dahlias
Oskar Kokoschka—Tempest

Der Blaue Reiter (c. 1909 – 1913)

The name means the Blue Rider, title of a Kandinsky picture. Group of Munich artists led by Wassily Kandinsky who totally discarded representation. By using bright colors and free brushwork he created a completely nonobjective style.

Wassily Kandinsky—Accompanied Contrast
Paul Klee—Fish Magic
Franz Marc—The Fate of Animals

Cubism (c. 1907 – 1914)

Subject matter broken up into a series of flat planes and basic geometric shapes and arranged in complex interlocking and overlapping relationships; multiple sides of an object were shown at the same time.

Juan Gris—La Table du Café, Abstraction in Gray
Pablo Picasso—Ambroise Vollard
Georges Braque—The Musician's Table
Fernand Léger—The City
Jacques Lipchitz—Man with Mandolin

Orphism

Developed by Robert Delaunay, it retained geometric patterns of Cubism, but used brighter colors and avoided the depiction of recognizable subject matter, as in Delaunay's *Circular Forms.*

Dadaism (c. 1916 – 1922)

Dada emerged as a protest against the violence and destruction of World War I; broke all the rules and traditions of art and society; nonsense, absurdity, and antiart prevailed in the works of the Dadaists; opened the way for invention and creativity; art no longer was dependent on manual craftsmanship or established rules.

Marcel Duchamp—To be looked at (from the other side of the glass), with one eye, close to, for almost an hour
Hans Arp—Collage with Squares Arranged According to the Laws of Chance

From *The Teacher's Book of Lists* © 1979, Goodyear Publishing Company, Inc.

Surrealism (c. 1924 – 1966)

Art based on dreams, the unconscious, and fantasy; paintings characterized by the juxtaposition of seemingly irrelevant and unrelated images often realistically reproduced, but placed in unexpected situations.

Max Ernst—Swamp Angel
Salvador Dali—Mae West
Joan Miró—Person Throwing a Stone at a Bird
René Magritte—Man with Newspaper

Abstract Expressionism

A method of painting, rather than a style, which began in the 1940s; images and colors are painted on the canvas in a random and spontaneous way; products of these painters differed—ranged from the drip painting of Pollock to the broad slashing brushstrokes of de Kooning; painters shared a primary interest in the process of applying paint rather than in recognizable subject matter.

Jackson Pollock—One
William de Kooning—Woman and Bicycle
Franz Kline—Painting No. 7
Mark Rothko—No. 10

Pop Art

A movement that originated in the United States during the late 1950s; the everyday environment of Americans—comic books, advertisements, and mass-produced products—provided the subject matter for Pop artists.

George Segal—Cinema
Jasper Johns—Three Flags
Claes Oldenburg—Soft Scissors
Robert Rauschenberg—Hot Dog
Andy Warhol—Coca Cola Bottles

Op Art

A movement in abstract art that developed in the United States around 1960, at about the same time as Pop but in a different direction; characterized by optical illusions and impressions of movement.

From *The Teacher's Book of Lists* © 1979 Goodyear Publishing Company, Inc.

Joseph Albers—Fugue
Bridget Riley—White Disks II
Victor Vasarely—Vega
Richard Anuskiewicz—Entrance to Green

Minimal Art

This art lacks personal involvement and tactile qualities of the works of the Abstract Expressionists; work characterized by smooth surfaces, pure color, simple geometric forms, and mechanical precision.

Ellsworth Kelly—Red Blue Green
Frank Stella—Empress of India
Kenneth Noland—Via Blues

ART FORMS

The following common art forms and media are often part of a classroom art program. The examples of works for use in children's art experiences are usually obtainable from art books, postcards, and inexpensive prints.

Sculpture

Alexander Archipenko—Woman Combing Her Hair
Umberto Boccioni—Unique Forms of Continuity in Space
Michelangelo Buonaratti—La Pietà
Alberto Giacometti—Man Pointing
Aristide Maillol—Mediterranean
Henry Moore—Reclining Figure
Rodin—The Burghers of Calais

Mosaics

Marc Chagall—Knesset, Jerusalem

Tapestries

Marc Chagall—Knesset, Jerusalem

Murals

Marc Chagall—Lincoln Art Center, New York
Jose Clemente Orozco—Catharsis, Palace of Fine Arts, Mexico City
Diego Rivera—Stairway in the National Palace, Mexico City
David Alfaro Siqueiros—Elements, National Preparatory School, Mexico City

Stained Glass

Marc Chagall—U.N. Building, New York; Hadassah Synogogue, Jerusalem

Paper Cutouts

Henri Matisse—Parakeet and Siren

Collage

Georges Braque—Bach
Pablo Picasso—Guitar
Kurt Schwitters—Disjointed Forces

Pastel

Mary Cassatt—Mother Feeding a Child
Jean Chardin—Self Portrait with Spectacles
Edgar Degas—The Tub
Quentin Latour—Mademoiselle Fel

Woodblock Printing

Albrecht Dürer—The Four Horsemen
  of the Apocalypse
Paul Gauguin—Offerings of Gratitude
Japanese and Chinese Woodblock Prints

Use of Line

Albrecht Dürer—All woodcuts
Jean Ingres—The Guillon—Lethière Family

Mobiles

Alexander Calder—Heads and Tails

Watercolor

John Sell Cotman—Greta Bridge
Alexander Cozens—View from Mirabella
Winslow Homer—Sloop Bermuda
John Marin—The Singer Building
Andrew Wyeth—Delphinium

ART VOCABULARY

armature—Skeletonlike framework upon which any type of media can be hung or modeled.

Art Nouveau—A widespread movement in architecture and design that spanned from the second half of the 19th century to the outbreak of World War I. Two major styles appear within Art Nouveau—one characterized by curving, twisting lines and asymmetry, as in the works of Aubrey Beardsley, Louis Comfort Tiffany, and Antoni Gaudi; the other by severe geometry and reductive ornamentation exemplified by Charles Rennie Mackintosh and J.M. Olbrich.

bas-relief (low relief)—Sculpture carved so as to project from a flat background as on a coin.

Bauhaus—School of design founded by Walter Gropius in Germany in 1919, closed by Hitler; combined all the arts, from applied arts to fine arts, with the materials and techniques of modern technology.

brayer—A rubber roller used for inking printing blocks.

broken color—Application of short strokes or small dabs of paint beside each other, which viewed from a distance blend together to form a new color.

calligraphy—Beautiful or decorative handwriting; a design created by the arrangement of letters to form a pattern.

caricature—A drawing that exaggerates the features of a person.

cartoon—A full-scale drawing on paper from which a painting, especially murals, are made. Also designates humorous drawings such as comic strips, caricatures, or political satires.

chiaroscuro—An Italian word meaning light and dark. Refers to the manner in which a painter handles atmospheric effects by use of values, tones, or light and dark shading.

chroma—The intensity or purity of a color.

collage—A composition made by pasting scraps of various material such as newspaper, wallpaper, photographs, and fabric on a flat surface.

cloisonné (cloy-zoh-nay')—An enameling process in which cells made of metal strips or wire are filled with colored enamels and baked or fired in a kiln.

complementary colors—Colors that are opposite each other on a color wheel, such as red and green; when mixed together the original intensities are grayed or neutralized.

contour—The line bounding a figure or object, creating an illusion of mass; outline.

crosshatch—A shading made by two sets of parallel lines crossing over each other, most often used in drawing and printing.

facade—Usually the front of a building.

fixative—A transparent varnish which is sprayed on pencil, chalk, or charcoal drawings to prevent smudging.

foreshortening—A method of reducing, often with distortion, parts of an object not parallel to the picture plane in order to convey depth and dimension.

fresco—Italian word for fresh. The technique of painting on wet plaster with pigments mixed with water. Paint is absorbed by the plaster and becomes chemically bound to it. Dry fresco (fresco secco) uses the same paint on dry plaster. Can also mean painting done in either manner.

frottage—A reproduction of a relief surface made by covering it with paper and rubbing it with pencil, pastel, crayon, etc. Also called a rubbing.

genre painting—A work that depicts a scene from everyday life.

gesso (jess'-oh)—A mixture of plaster and glue, or gypsum, used to prepare a surface for painting.

gouache (goo-ahsh')—An opaque watercolor made by adding white to a transparent watercolor.

hue—The name of a color—red, blue, etc.

impasto—Paint applied thickly by a brush or knife.

kinetic art—All art forms in which movement appears to take place or actually does take place, often induced by the effect of light. See works by Abraham Palatnik, Nicolas Schöffer, and Victor Vasarely.

line—An invention of man used to delineate the contour of an object and to define space.

lithography—Printmaking process in which a design is drawn onto a polished stone or metal plate with an oily crayon or other greasy material. After moistening the entire surface, ink is applied which adheres only to the lines drawn.

mass—Shapes or forms; volume or area, as opposed to space.

monochromatic color—The different values or intensities of one color.

mosaic—Designs or pictures made by setting small pices of material—glass, marble, or stones—in concrete or plaster, on surfaces such as walls or floors.

montage—A composition made by fitting together pictures or parts of pictures. In motion pictures, it refers to a rapid sequence of images or pictures.

mural—A large painting done directly on a wall or done separately and affixed to a wall.

negative space—The space around objects or shapes.

opaque—Nontransparent.

palette—A thin board or tablet on which colors are placed and mixed. Also refers to the colors used by an artist or group of artists.

pastel—Ground pigments compressed into a chalklike stick. Also, work done in this medium.

pointillism—A painting technique in which a series of small dots of pure color are systematically placed next to each other; also referred to as Divisionism.

primary colors—The three basic colors from which most other colors are made: red, yellow, and blue.

rhythm—The recurrence or repetition of features or objects in a work of art.

secondary colors—Colors containing equal amounts of two primary colors: orange, violet, and green.

sgraffito—A design made by scratching through a surface layer such as glaze or plaster to reveal a different-colored surface beneath.

shade—A darker value of a color, obtained by mixing black to the hue.

shape—The contours of a form of an object.

symmetry—A balance achieved by the arrangement of forms on both sides of an imaginary axis.

terra cotta—An Italian word for cooked-earth. Reddish brown clay used for pottery, sculpture, or building material.

tertiary colors—Colors produced by mixing a primary with a secondary hue: red-orange, blue-green, yellow-green.

tesserae—Small pieces of glass or stone used in making mosaics.

texture—The surface of a work of art—rough, smooth, shiny.

tint—A light value achieved by adding white to a hue.

trompe-l'oeil (trohmp-loy')—French word for "deceive the eye"; a type of painting in which the objects depicted appear to be real.

triptych—A three-paneled picture, carving, or work of art.

value—The lightness or darkness of a color.

vanishing point—The point on the horizon toward which parallel lines appear to converge.

wash—A thin, transparent film of color, usually watercolor or ink.

COLOR WORDS

Reds	Browns	Yellows	Purples	Whites
carmine	beige	amber	fuchsia	alabaster
cerise	bronze	buff	heliotrope	cream
cherry	chocolate	canary	lavender	ivory
coral	cinnamon	champagne	lilac	pearl
crimson	coffee	eggshell	magenta	
damask	ecru	gold	maroon	
pink	fawn	lemon	mauve	
rose	hazel	ocher	plum	
ruby	henna	saffron	violet	
salmon	khaki	xanthic		
scarlet	mahogany			
titian	puce			
vermillion	sienna			
	tan			
	taupe			
	tawny			
	umber			

Oranges	Greens	Blues	Blacks
apricot	chartreuse	aquamarine	ebony
copper	emerald	azure	raven
peach	lime	bice	sable
rust	reseda	cerulean	silver
tangerine		indigo	slate
		sapphire	
		turquoise	

Color Word Activities

1. Arrange the hues in each color group from light to dark by making a list, painting samples of the colors, or attaching to a sheet of paper samples from fabric, thread, magazines, clothing catalogs, paint chip samples, or nature.

2. Make lists of color words that describe colors by naming objects. These objects can either be added as adjectives or be the names of the colors themselves.

   pea green   periwinkle blue   avocado green   fire engine red
   salmon   peach   fawn

3. List colors that could fit into more than one major color category.

   rust—Is it brown or orange?   coral—Is it red or orange?
   puce—Is it red or brown?   chartreuse—Is it yellow or green?

4. Experiment with paint to develop formulas for various hues.

   1 part yellow + 2 parts orange = _____

   Measure parts by a teaspoon, drops from a straw, or a medicine dropper.

5. Describe colors using words.

   chartreuse—a bright greenish-yellow
   reseda—a dull grayish-green
   slate—dark grayish-blue

6. Use paint catalogues or color charts to find and list color names. See which of these are not in the dictionary. Tell which of these words you think may someday enter the dictionary due to common use in everyday language.

From *The Teacher's Book of Lists* © 1979, Goodyear Publishing Company, Inc.

MUSICAL PERIODS

Pre-17th Century

Characterized by the development of instruments, notation system, major diatonic scale, and five-lined staff.

Orlando Di Lasso—the height of Renaissance music, religious as well as Italian madrigals and chansons

Giovanni Pierluigi di Palestrina—prominent at the height of Renaissance music; one of the greatest composers of church music—Missa Papae Marcelli (Marcellus Mass)

17th Century

This was a period of great musical progress; generally thought of as the beginning of modern music.

Baroque Period: late 1500s to middle 1700s

Began with a rebellion against the polyphony of Renaissance music, except in the form of counterpoint; grand and brilliant music; rich display of color with contrasting effects between slow and fast, solo and chorus, loud and soft; masses of ornamentation, sometimes excessively exaggerated; elaborate harmonics; often massive effects of voices and instruments; attempted a display of virtuosity.

Johann Sebastian Bach—called the father of modern music
>   Magnificat (organ music)
>   Brandenburg Concertos
>   Prelude and Fugue in D Major
>   Fantasia and Fugue in G Minor
>   St. Matthew Passion (cantata)
>   B Minor Mass
>   The Well-Tempered Clavier

George Frederick Handel
>   Fireworks Music
>   The Beggar's Opera
>   The Messiah (oratorio)

Jean-Baptiste Lully—founder of French opera
>   Le Bourgeois Gentilhomme—The Middle-Class Nobleman—composed with Molière
>   Alceste (opera)

From *The Teacher's Book of Lists* © 1979, Goodyear Publishing Company, Inc.

Claudio Monteverdi—a bridge between Renaissance and the Baroque
    Orfeo (opera)
    Hear the Murmuring Waters (from Book II of madrigals)

Henry Purcell—England's greatest composer
    "Dido's Lament" from Dido and Aeneas (opera)
    Golden Sonata in F

Alessandro Scarlatti
    Il Tigrane (opera)
    Il Trionfo del l'onore—The Triumph of Honor (comic opera)

Domenico Scarlatti—remembered for harpsichord compositions; called the father of modern keyboard technique
    Sonate Pastorale

"Rococo" Period: the last thirty to forty years of the Baroque period

A transition period into the Classical; light, highly ornamented style.

Karl Philipp Emanuel Bach
    Solfeggietto

Antonio Vivaldi
    The Seasons, Op. 8 (Le quattro stagione)
    La Stravaganza, Op. 4 (twelve concertos)

Classical Period: middle 1700s to early 1800s

Reflected the ideal of an impersonal, natural concept of beauty; displayed definite patterns with strict adherence to structure and balance; elegant, formal and restrained; significant instrumental development (clarinet, trumpet, hunting horn, piano)

Luigi Boccherini
    Minuet from String Quartet, Op. 13, No. 4

Muzio Clementi
    Gradus ad Parnassum—Steps to Parnassus, 100 piano études, still used by many piano students

Christopher Willibald Gluck
    Orfeo ed Euridice
    Alceste
    Don Juan (ballet)

Joseph Haydn
    London Symphonies
    Toy Symphony
    The Creation (oratorio)

The Seasons (oratorio)
Farewell Symphony

Wolfgang Amadeus Mozart
The Marriage of Figaro (opera)
Don Giovanni (opera)
The "Jupiter" Symphony (Symphony #41 in C Major)

Ludwig Van Beethoven—Often called the bridge between the Classical and Romantic periods; a pioneer figure whose compositions bear characteristics of both periods, yet were uniquely individual; demonstrated that music could reveal the composer's character and be more than impersonal and stylized in definite patterns; brought the symphony to its most perfect stage of development; perhaps the most outstanding composer of western music.

Eroica (Third Symphony)
Fifth Symphony, in C Minor
Pastoral (Sixth Symphony)
Ninth Symphony (contains a choral finale)
Emperor Concerto (#5 in Eb major, op. 73)
Pathétique Sonata
Moonlight Sonata
Fidelio (Beethoven's only opera)
Violin Concerto

Romantic Period: early 1800s to late 1800s

Characterized by music freed of rigid structures; expressed emotion and revealed composers' individuality; often used to tell a story and portray events and scenes; music began to be identified with the country of the composer.

(Italy) *Giacomo Puccini*
La Bohème (opera)
Tosca (opera)
Madame Butterfly (opera)

Gioacchino Rossini
William Tell (opera)
The Barber of Seville (opera)
Peteti Messe solunnelle (Short Solemn Mass)

Giuseppe Verdi
Aïda (opera)
La Traviata (opera)

From *The Teacher's Book of Lists* © 1979, Goodyear Publishing Company, Inc.

(Germany-Austria) *Johannes Brahms*
>A German Requiem
>First Symphony
>Variations on a Theme by Haydn

Felix Mendelssohn
>Midsummer's Night Dream
>Hebrides Overture (Fingal's Cave)
>"Spring Song"—No. 30 from Songs Without Words (collection of piano pieces)

Franz Schubert—famous as greatest composer of "lieder," German art-songs
>Gretchen at the Spinning Wheel
>The Erl-King
>Unfinished Symphony
>Rosamunde Music
>C Major Symphony (The Great)

Robert Schumann
>Piano Concerto in A Minor
>Humoresque
>Abegg Variations

Johann Strauss (the Younger)
>Die Fledermaus (opera)
>Tales from the Vienna Woods

Richard Wagner
>Tristan and Isolde (opera)
>Tannhäuser (opera)
>The Ring of the Nibelung (opera)

(France) *Hector Berlioz*
>Roman Carnival Overture
>Fantastic Symphony
>The Childhood of Christ (oratorio)
>"Rákóczi March" from The Damnation of Faust

Georges Bizet
>Carmen (opera)
>Children's Games (pieces for piano duet)

Camille Saint-Saëns
>The Carnival of the Animals
>Danse macabre (Dance of Death)
>Cello Concerto No. 1

(Hungary) *Franz Liszt*
    Hungarian Rhapsodies
    Mephisto Waltz
    Prometheus (symphonic poem)

(Poland) *Frédéric Chopin*
    Minute Waltz (Waltz in Db, Op. 64, No. 1)
    Military Polonaise (Polonaise in A, Op. 40, No. 1)
    Prelude in A, Op. 28, No. 7
    Prelude in C Minor, Op. 28, No. 20

(Bohemia) *Anton Dvořák*
    New World Symphony
    Slavonic Rhapsodies

Bedřich Smetana
    My Country (six symphonic tone poems)
    From My Life (string quartet)

(Russia) *Modest Moussorgsky*
    Boris Godunov (opera)
    Songs and Dances of Death

Nikolai Rimsky-Korsakov
    Scheherazade (symphonic suite)
    The Russian Easter Overture

Piotr (Peter) Ilyich Tchaikovsky
    The Nutcracker Suite (ballet)
    Swan Lake (ballet)
    Sleeping Beauty (ballet)
    1812 Overture
    Pathétique Symphony
    Romeo and Juliet (overture-fantasy)
    First Piano Concerto

(Norway) *Edvard Grieg*
    Peer Gynt Suite

(United States) *Edward MacDowell*
    Indian Suite
    Woodland Sketches
    The Tragica Sonata

John Philip Sousa
    Semper Fidelis
    The Washington Post March

From *The Teacher's Book of Lists* © 1979, Goodyear Publishing Company, Inc.

Modern Period: late 1800s to middle 1900s

This was music generally written to escape the romantic tradition, the expected, and the commonplace: neoclassicism—an attempt to apply the modern concepts of rhythm and tonality to the classic forms; impressionism—expression of the reaction of the senses to nature, events, and emotions; beauty of tone, rich use of color, whole-tone scale, and new harmonic devices; often programmatic, intended to transmit specific meaning to the listener; experimentalism—music involving atonality, bitonality, tone clusters, and other experimental concepts; some use of electronic instruments

Béla Bartók
> String quartets
> Mikrokosmos (children's piano pieces)

Claude Debussy
> The Afternoon of a Faun
> "Iberia" from Images
> Children's Corner

George Gershwin
> Rhapsody in Blue
> An American in Paris (symphonic poem)
> Piano Concerto in F

Paul Hindemith
> Suite 1922
> When Lilacs Last in the Dooryard Bloom'd (based on a poem by Walt Whitman)

Charles Ives
> Concord Sonata
> Three Places in New England
> A Symphony: Holidays

Sergei Prokofiev
> Classical Symphony
> Peter and the Wolf
> Alexander Nevsky (cantata)
> Scythian Suite

Maurice Ravel
> Spanish Rhapsody
> Daphnis and Chloe (ballet)
> Fountains (Jeux d'eau)

Arnold Schoenberg
> Five Orchestral Pieces, Op. 23
> A Survivor of Warsaw
> Pierrot Lunaire (Pierrot by Moonlight)

From *The Teacher's Book of Lists* © 1979 Goodyear Publishing Company, Inc.

Richard Strauss
> Der Rosenkavalier (opera)
> Aus Italien (From Italy)

Igor Stravinsky
> Petrushka (ballet)
> The Firebird (ballet)
> Symphony of Psalms
> The Rite of Spring (ballet)
> Ragtime for Eleven Instruments (jazz)

Contemporary Period: middle 1900s to present

Characterized by continuing experimentalism; some attempts to reconcile neoclassicism with some experimentalist ideas; new and exciting uses of instruments, fresh tone qualities and structures.

Benjamin Britten
> The Young Person's Guide to the Orchestra
> Peter Grimes (opera)
> Spring Symphony

Aaron Copland
> Rodeo (ballet)
> Billy the Kid (ballet)
> Appalachian Spring (ballet)

Dmitri Shostakovich
> Symphony No. 1
> The Nose (opera)
> Katerina Ismailova (opera)

Karl-Heinz Stockhausen—one of the pioneers of electronic music
> Zeitmasse (Measures of Time)
> Momente (Moments)
> Microphonie I

Heitor Villa-Lobos
> Bachiana brazileiras, No. 5
> Chôros

From The Teacher's Book of Lists © 1979, Goodyear Publishing Company, Inc.

MUSICAL FORMS

This list of musical forms is grouped according to the general period of their development or perfection. A suggested example for listening follows each form.

Middle Ages: religious music

chants (plainsongs)—single melodic lines sung by a group; later became polyphonic (two or more melodies woven together)

Gregorian chants, Ambrosian chants

Middle Ages: secular music

folk music
canons (rounds) of the minstrels and troubadours
Summer Is Icumen In (one of the earliest canons, 13th century)

Renaissance

madrigal—in the 14th century, a poem set to music in two voice-parts; by the 16th century, often very fine, free-form poetry, still in counterpoint, although later developing into more chordal forms; eventually developing into one-, two-, three-, and four-part cantatas

Now Is the Month of Maying, Thomas Morley

The Swan Song, Orlando Gibbons

motet—vocal music sung by a group, usually two-part, without orchestral accompaniment, in strict rhythm; later, more parts were added until, by the mid-16th century, the motet became the sacred counterpart of the madrigal

Motets by Palestrina and J.S. Bach

Baroque Period: musical forms

chorale prelude—music based on a chorale melody, composed for the organ

Three Chorales for Organ, César Franck (examples of chorale preludes, although not of the Baroque Period)

concerto grosso—a sonata for several solo instruments (often two violins and a cello) alternating with full orchestra

Brandenburg Concertos, J.S. Bach

dance suite (partita)—short, contrasting dance movements; four usual movements were the allemande, courante, saraband, and gigue

J.S. Bach wrote six French suites, six English suites, and six partitas

fugue—a melody carried on in several overlapping voices

The Art of the Fugue, J.S. Bach

passacaglia (chaconne)—slow and stately dance suite, usually in triple meter
Passacaglia in C Minor, J.S. Bach

rondo—music with a theme that recurs in its original key at certain intervals; later, often used as last movements in compositions by Haydn, Mozart, Beethoven

Last movement of Piano Sonata in A, K. 331, Wolfgang Amadeus Mozart

toccata—keyboard composition with elaborate and rapid passage work, such as runs and arpeggios

Toccata and Fugue in D Minor, J.S. Bach

Toccatas, Girolamo Frescobaldi

trio sonata—in this early development, the sonata was music of a single two- or three-part movement, usually with three voice-parts performed by four instruments

Golden Sonata in F, Henry Purcell

Baroque Period: vocal forms

cantata—short version of the oratorio, usually written on secular themes
Suddenly, Shall the Day Appear, Paul Hindemith
Cantata No. 140—Wachet Auf, J.S. Bach

chorale—a simple hymn, enlarged and ornamented for instruments; later expanded and used in church cantatas

A Mighty Fortress Is Our God, Martin Luther

grand opera—generally applied to early Italian operas and later works with involved, serious plots; also, today applied to operas with lavish productions

Aïda, Giuseppe Verdi (example of grande opera, although not of the Baroque Period)

opera—a drama performed by singing, with costumes, scenery, action, and orchestral accompaniment (some later operas employed ballet groups, also)

Carmen, Georges Bizet (example of opera, although not of the Baroque Period)

oratorio—of religious nature, usually with scriptural text; tells a story; for voices with orchestral accompaniment; usually no action, scenery, or costumes

The Messiah, George Frederick Handel

From *The Teacher's Book of Lists* © 1979, Goodyear Publishing Company, Inc.

Classical Period

concerto—sonata for solo instrument with orchestral accompaniment, usually of the following three movements: (1) sonata form, (2) movement in a slower tempo, (3) lively rondo, theme with variations, or again, a movement in sonata form

Concerto No. 1 in Bb Minor, Peter Ilyich Tchaikovsky

chamber music—sonata written for instrumental groupings, such as the string quartet or woodwind quintet, to be performed in a small place

Trout Quintet, Franz Schubert

sonata—developed into a major composition for solo instrument (occasionally two or three may be used) of the following four sections: (1) the allegro, fast movement, (2) a slow movement, (3) a minuet or scherzo, sometimes omitted, (4) a finale, usually fast

Pathétique Sonata, Ludwig van Beethoven

sonata-allegro form—a significant development of the period, used as the first movement of sonatas, symphonies, overtures, and chamber works, with the following sections: (1) statement of a theme, (2) development of theme at length, (3) restatement of original theme

First movement from Sonata, Op. 2, No. 1, Beethoven

symphony—sonata for full symphony orchestra; nearly every major composer wrote at least one symphony

Symphony No. 8 in B Minor (Unfinished), Franz Schubert

Romantic Period

art songs ("lieder")—songs with music composed to fit the text of romantic poetry, often without repetition of stanzas and refrains as in folk songs

Mullerlieder and *Gretchen Am Spinnrade,* Franz Schubert

ballet—a story told in dancing; music written for ballet is frequently used in concerts

Giselle, Adolphe Adam

comic opera (sometimes called operetta and light opera)—lighter, less serious, usually shorter version of the opera form; usually includes speaking roles

The Student Prince, Sigmund Romberg

concert overture—resembles the overture to an opera but is meant to be played in a concert hall as an independent composition

Academic Festival Overture, Johannes Brahms

music-dramas—Richard Wagner's strong, cyclical operas demanding more staging, vocal stamina, and physical endurance than earlier operas

Tristan and Isolde, Richard Wagner

symphonic poem (called tone poem in the Modern Period)—a single symphonic picture, without separate movements, in which the music usually follows a story
Romeo and Juliet (symphonic poem)—Peter Ilyich Tchaikovsky
Don Quixote (tone poem)—Richard Strauss

symphonic suite (program symphony)—lighter version of the symphony, consisting of sections that are related through a chain of events or story
Scheherazade, Nicolai Rimsky-Korsakov

Some Other Forms

aleatory music—music incorporating the element of chance; not all the pitches or rhythms are specified; performers may introduce random elements; no two performances are alike
Stockhausen, Cage (composers)

étude—an instrumental composition designed to help improve the player's techniques
Revolutionary Étude, Chopin

fantasia—a work in free form, according to the composer's desires, not following a strict scheme, although often versions of more standard forms
Wanderer Fantasie in C, Schubert

free form—may not follow any conventional succession of themes; composer then works for unity with harmonization and orchestration
Jeux (Games), Debussy

march—music with a strong rhythm and regular phrases, usually in 2/4 or 4/4 time, suitable for accompanying a marching group
John Philip Sousa's marches

overture—a composition that introduces a longer work, such as an opera or oratorio
Overture on Hebrew Themes, Prokofiev

rhapsody—a free form, relatively short composition, expressing a particular mood
Rhapsody on a Theme by Paganini, Rachmaninoff

scherzo—a movement from a sonata, usually involving an element of surprise; or an independent piece of music that is serious and dramatic rather than playful
Chopin, Brahms

serenade—an instrumental composition for a small group of instruments, usually consisting of several movements
A Little Night Music, Mozart

theme and variations—a series of different treatments of a theme, with key changes, altered rhythm and tempo, or other elements for some of the variations
Variations on a Theme by Handel, Brahms

From *The Teacher's Book of Lists* © 1979, Goodyear Publishing Company, Inc.

MUSIC VOCABULARY

a cappella—singing without instrumental accompaniment

accent—an emphasis that makes one note of a measure sound more important than others

arpeggio—a series of chord tones, played in quick succession

bar—*see* measure

chord—tones sounded together; usually refers to three or more tones

coda—a concluding section added after the main piece is finished

counterpoint—combination of two or more melodies, played together, but retaining each one's identity

downbeat—the first accented beat in a measure

dynamics—the contrasts and progressions between the loudness and softness of the music (*see* Dynamics Marks, page 208)

embellishment—*see* ornament

expression—the feeling or mood to be conveyed by the music; expression marks, added by the composer, give the performer detailed directions on how to play (*see* Expression Marks, page 207)

fifth—an interval of five steps between tones; fifth note of a scale

form—the structure of the musical composition

glissando—a "slide"; moving rapidly up or down the scale by sliding a finger along a string, on stringed instruments, or keys, on a piano

harmonics—faint, flutelike sounds of string instruments produced by lightly touching a string, rather than pressing firmly

harmony—the combining of tones; the study of chord combinations and progressions

homophony—a single melody, with its accompanying chords and harmony

improvise—to make up melodies and harmonies while singing or playing, without a preconceived plan

incidental music—music added to a play or film to set a mood or add excitement

interval—the difference (distance) between the pitch of two sounds

key—the "home" center of a musical work; the scale or series of tones whose center (point of rest) is the key name

libretto—the text of the words to be sung in an opera, oratorio, or musical play

measure (bar)—a unit of time in music with a given number of beats

melody—a succession of notes with a definite pattern

ornament (embellishment)—decorations of the melody (grace notes, trills, etc.)

pitch—sound of a musical tone, either high or low; relation of one tone to another

polyphony—*see* counterpoint

rhythm—the arrangement in music of accented and unaccented, long and short, sounds

scale—a series of tones leading from one tone to its octave; the most common scales are major, minor, chromatic, and whole tone

staff—the lines and spaces on which notes are written

syncopation—a shifting of the accent (usually on the first beat of a measure) to one of the weaker beats in the measure

tempo (time)—the rate of speed of the music

third—third note of a scale; an interval of three steps whose tones are written on adjacent lines of adjacent spaces of the staff

timbre (tone color)—quality of tone; the characteristic sound of specific instruments or of the voice

time—*see* tempo

tonality—the quality of belonging to a definite key

tone—a sound with a definite pitch

tone color—*see* timbre

treble—the higher range of sounds

EXPRESSION AND TEMPO MARKS

accelerando (accel.)—becoming quicker (opposite of ritardando)

adagio—slow and leisurely

allegro—quick and cheerful

andante—slowly; gently moving; walking tempo

brillante—bright; sparkling

cantabile—like a singing tone

dolce—sweetly

giocoso—gaily; cheerfully

grave—slow; solemn

largo—very slow; broad; stately

legato—smoothly connected (opposite of staccato)

lento—slowly; between andante and largo

From *The Teacher's Book of Lists* © 1979, Goodyear Publishing Company, Inc.

maestoso—majestically

moderato—at a moderate, even pace

presto—very quickly; faster than allegro

risoluto—boldly; resolute

ritardando (ritard.)—becoming slower (opposite of accelerando)

semplice—simply

sostenuto—sustained

staccato—sharp, short notes (opposite of legato)

tranquillo—calm; peaceful

un poco (a poco)—a little

vigoroso—boldly

vivace—quick and lively; faster than allegro

vivo—animated

Some Other Marks

agitato	expressivo	rigore
allargando	giusto	ritenuto
allegreto	incalzando	rotondo
allegro (molto) brioso	largamente	rubato
andantino	leggiero	sognando
animato	lento doloroso	solemne
appassionata	marcato	spirito
calando	morendo	subito
con brio	moto	tanto
energico	pesante	tempestoso

MUSICAL SYMBOLS

Dynamics Marks

very loud $f\!f$

loud (forte) f

fairly loud $m\!f$

sforzando (play with sudden force) $s\!f$ $s\!f\!z$

fairly soft mp

soft (piano) p

very soft pp

crescendo (gradually) ◁

getting louder cresc.

decrescendo (gradually) getting softer   decr.

diminuendo (gradually) getting softer   dim.

accent marks > ∧

accented notes

Other Musical Symbols

staff   bar   double bars

2 3 4 6 9   time (meter) signatures—top number indicates number of beats per measure;
4 4 4 8 8   bottom number indicates the kind of note that receives one beat

$\frac{2}{4}$ = two beats per measure; quarter note receives one beat

common time $\frac{4}{4}$ **C**

cut time (alla breve); two beats per measure; one beat to each half note ¢

Note Values

whole note **O**

half note

quarter note

eighth note

sixteenth note

triplets—play in the same time as two notes of the same value

grace note—play quickly; no time value

dotted quarter note
a dot increases the note value by half

treble clef sign (C clef)

bass clef sign (F clef)

fermata—hold or prolong beyond the allotted time ⌒

sustained (held a bit longer) note

tie; play the first note and hold it through the second note; second note is not played

Equivalent Rests

whole rest

half rest

quarter rest

eighth rest

sixteenth rest

From The Teacher's Book of Lists © 1979, Goodyear Publishing Company, Inc.

staccato note and chord—play in a short, detached way

staccatissimo—very short and detached

phrase—to be played or sung smoothly, to show they belong together in conveying meaning

slur—a phrase to be sung or played very smoothly

trill—rapidly alternating two adjoining notes of the scale *tr*

flat—lower the note one half step ♭

sharp—raise the note one half step ♯

double flat—lower the note two half steps ♭♭

double sharp—raise the note two half steps

natural—cancel out a given sharp or flat ♮

first ending |1.

second ending |2.

repeat :‖

da capo al fine—return to the beginning of the piece, *D. C. al fine* and play to the word "fine"

pedal down *Ped*   pedal up ✳

up bow V   down bow ⊓

arpeggio—play each note of the chord, from low to high, in very rapid succession

---

MUSIC MAKERS—INSTRUMENTS AND VOICES

The Symphony Orchestra—number of instruments varies, usually 98-112 players

The String Choir (62-66)

Viol Family (bowed or plucked)

    violin 32-34

    viola 12

    violoncello (cello) 10

    double bass 8-10

unbowed strings (2-3)—sometimes placed in a miscellaneous category

    harp 1-2

    piano 1

The Woodwind Choir (16)

    All have reeds but the piccolo and flute, which have a hole to blow across

    piccolo 1—the highest range in the orchestra

flute 3
oboe* 3
English horn* 1
bassoon* 3
contra bassoon* 1—the lowest range in the orchestra
clarinet 3
bass clarinet 1
saxophone—more recent origin, sometimes used by modern and contemporary composers as a solo instrument

*Have double reeds.

The Brass Choir (13-18)
All have cupped mouthpieces
trumpet 3-5
trombone 3-4
tuba 1
French horn 6-8

The Percussion Group (5-9)
Pitched
tympani (kettledrums) 2-4
xylophone
chimes   } 3-5
glockenspiel (bells)

Nonpitched

snare drum	bass drum
gong (tamtam)	triangle
cymbals	tambourine
woodblocks	castanets

Sometimes used with the symphony orchestra: Latin American rhythm instruments such as bongos, marimba, claves, and novelty instruments such as rattles, sandblocks, and sleighbells

Other Instrumental Groupings

Symphonic Band
Chamber Music Groups—string quartets and trios, woodwind quintets, etc.
Chamber Orchestra
Brass Band

From *The Teacher's Book of Lists* © 1979, Goodyear Publishing Company, Inc.

Marching Band
Jazz Band
Dance Band

Rock Band
Consort
Broken Consort

Steel Band
Military Band

Some Other Instruments

accordion
bagpipe
balalaika
banjo
baryton
bugle
calliope
chitarrone
chyn (ch'in)
clavichord
clavilux
concertina
crwth
curtal
dulcimer
fife
flageolet
flügelhorn

gittern
glass harmonica
guiro
guitar
gusle
hardanger fiddle
harmonica
harmonium
Hawaiian guitar
helicon
hornpipe
hurdy-gurdy
Irish harp
Jew's harp
kantele
kithara
koto
lur

lute
lyre
mandolin
maracas
marimba
mellophone
monochord
ocarina
oliphant
pandora
pipe
psaltery
qānūn
rabab
racket
rebec
saxhorn
serpent

shakuhachi
shamisen
sitar
spinet
tablas
tambura
theorbo
timbrel
tom-tom
Turkish crescent
'ud
ukulele
vielle
vina
zampogna
zither

Occasionally Used in the Orchestra

basset horn
celesta
cornet
euphonium
harpsichord
heckelphone

oboe do caccia
oboe d'amore
ophicleide
recorder
vibraharp (vibes)

Electronic Instruments

(Instruments fitted with electronic devices, although sound is produced in the usual manner—guitars, flutes, double basses, violins, violas, cellos, saxophones, pianos, harpsichords)

chord organ
combo organ
electronic organ (Hammond organ)

novachord
ondes Martenot
theremin

Instruments at Least 2,000 Years Old That Are Still Played Today

bagpipe	finger cymbals	panpipes	shofar
castanets	Jew's harp	shawn	tambourine
chyn	lyre	sheng	vina

Voice Ranges

Men's voices from low to high:
  bass
  baritone
  tenor

Women's voices from low to high:
  alto (contralto)
  mezzo-soprano
  soprano

Operatic sopranos:
  coloratura soprano
  dramatic soprano
  lyric soprano

Male soprano parts:
  boy soprano
  falsetto

Bass singers:
  basso buffo
  basso cantante
  basso profondo

Male alto:
  countertenor

Singing Forms and Styles

aria
art song
ballad
barcarole
calypso
carol
chantey (shanty)
folk song
lullaby

popular song
recitative
scatting
song
spiritual
sprechstimme
troubadour
trouvère
yodel

From *The Teacher's Book Of Lists* ©1979, Goodyear Publishing Company, Inc.

eleven
LITERATURE

GREEK AND ROMAN GODS AND GODDESSES

Greek Name	Roman Name	Role
Zeus	Jupiter ♃	King of the gods
Hera	Juno ⚡	Queen of the gods
Aphrodite	Venus ♀	Goddess of love
Ares	Mars ♂	God of war, wisdom, and crafts
Demeter	Ceres ⚹	Goddess of agriculture
Hades	Pluto ♇	God of the underworld
Hermes	Mercury ☿	Messenger of the gods
Hestia	Vesta ⚱	Goddess of hearth and home
Poseidon	Neptune ♆	God of the sea
Apollo	Apollo	God of sun, music, and medicine
Artemis	Diana	Goddess of the hunt
Asclepius	Aesculapius	God of medicine
Athena	Minerva	Goddess of wisdom
Chloris	Flora	Goddess of flowers
Dionysus	Bacchus	God of wine
Enyo	Bellona	Goddess of war
Eos	Aurora	Goddess of the dawn

Eros	Cupid	God of love
Gaea	Terra	Symbol of the earth
Hebe	Juventas	Goddess of youth and cupbearer to the gods
Hephaestus	Vulcan	God of fire and blacksmith to the gods
Hygeia	Salus	Goddess of health
Hypnos	Somnus	God of sleep
Iris		Goddess of the rainbow
	Janus	God of gates and doors and all beginnings
Morpheus		God of dreams
Nike	Victoria	Goddess of victory
Pan	Faunus	God of flocks, pastures, forests, and wildlife
Panacea		Goddess of healing
Persephone	Proserpina	Queen of the underworld
Rhea		Mother of the gods
Selene	Luna	Goddess of the moon
Thanatos	Mors	God of death
	Nox	Goddess of night

LITERARY AND MYTHOLOGICAL MONSTERS AND CREATURES

Argus—a hundred-eyed giant of Greek mythology

Centaur—Greek mythological monster, half man (from the waist up) and half horse (from the waist down)

Cerberus—a many-headed dog of Greek mythology

Chimera—a fire-breathing monster—part lion, part goat, part dragon—of Greek mythology

Cyclops—a race of one-eyed giants in Greek mythology

Dracula—a centuries-old vampire who was a corpse during the day but came to life at night; from a novel by Bram Stoker

Dragons—monsters famous in legends of many different countries

Frankenstein's monster—a manlike monster created by Dr. Frankenstein in the book of the same name by Mary Wollstonecraft Shelley

Giant—a huge, manlike monster

Gorgons—three female monsters of Greek mythology with serpents for hair

Griffin—a mythical creature, half eagle and half lion

Harpy—a dirty, winged monster with the head of a woman and the tail, legs, and talons of a bird

Hydra—Greek mythological monster; a nine-headed serpent which grew two heads for each one that was cut off

Jabberwock—the fabulous monster in the nonsense poem "Jabberwocky" in *Through the Looking Glass* by Lewis Carroll

Medusa—one of the Gorgons

Minotaur—from Greek mythology; a manlike monster with a bull's head

Pegasus—winged horse of Greek mythology

Phoenix—a legendary Egyptian bird

Roc—a very large, strong legendary bird believed to live in the area around the Indian Ocean

Sphinx—in Greek mythology, a monster with the head of a woman, body and paws of a lion, and huge birdlike wings

Titans—a group of earth giants from Greek mythology, said to have had immense size and brute strength

Unicorn—legendary beast, usually with the head and body of a horse, the hind legs of an antelope, the tail of a lion, and a single, long, sharp twisted horn in the middle of its forehead

Vampires—legendary ghosts which came out of their graves to attack the living

Werewolves—people thought to be transformed into wolves

NEWBERY AWARD WINNERS

The Newbery Medal was named after John Newbery, a famous 18th century seller of children's books. It was first given in 1921, by Frederic G. Melcher, as an incentive for better quality in children's books. The Medal is now donated annually by Daniel Melcher, son of the original donor, to the author of the most distinguished contribution to American literature for children published during the preceding year. Copies of the Newbery list, as well as the Caldecott list that follows, can be given to parents to use as a reference for selecting books from the library, for gifts, or for the home.

1922 *The Story of Mankind.* Hendrik Willem van Loon. (Liveright)

1923 *The Voyages of Doctor Dolittle.* Hugh Lofting. (Lippincott)

1924 *The Dark Frigate.* Charles Hawes. (Little, Brown)

1925 *Tales from Silver Lands.* Charles Finger. (Doubleday)

1926 *Shen of the Sea.* Arthur Bowie Chrisman. (Dutton)

1927 *Smoky, the Cowhorse.* Will James. (Scribner)

1928 *Gayneck, the Story of a Pigeon.* Dhan Gopal Mukerji. (Dutton)

1929 *The Trumpeter of Krakow.* Eric P. Kelly. (Macmillan)

1930 *Hitty, Her First Hundred Years.* Rachael Field. (Macmillan)

1931 *The Cat Who Went to Heaven.* Elizabeth Coatsworth. (Macmillan)

1932 *Waterless Mountain.* Laura Adams Armer. (Longmans Green)

1933 *Young Fu of the Upper Yangtze.* Elizabeth Lewis. (Holt, Rinehart & Winston)

1934 *Invincible Louisa.* Cornelia Meigs. (Little, Brown)

1935 *Dobry.* Monica Shannon. (Viking)

1936 *Caddie Woodlawn.* Carol Brink. (Macmillan)

1937 *Roller Skates.* Ruth Sawyer. (Viking)

1938 *The White Stag.* Kate Seredy. (Viking)

1939 *Thimble Summer.* Elizabeth Enright. (Holt, Rinehart & Winston)

1940 *Daniel Boone.* James Daugherty. (Viking)

1941 *Call It Courage.* Armstrong Sperry. (Macmillan)

1942 *The Matchlock Gun.* Walter D. Edmonds. (Dodd, Mead)

1943 *Adam of the Road.* Elizabeth Janet Gray. (Viking)

1944 *Johnny Tremaine.* Esther Forbes. (Houghton Mifflin)

1945 *Rabbit Hill.* Robert Lawson. (Viking)

From *The Teacher's Book of Lists* © 1979, Goodyear Publishing Company, Inc.

1946   *Strawberry Girl.* Lois Lenski. (Lippincott)

1947   *Miss Hickory.* Carolyn Sherwin Bailey. (Viking)

1948   *The Twenty-One Balloons.* William Pene du Bois. (Viking)

1949   *King of the Wind.* Marguerite Henry. (Rand McNally)

1950   *The Door in the Wall.* Marguerite de Angeli. (Doubleday)

1951   *Amos Fortune, Free Man.* Elizabeth Yates. (Aladdin)

1952   *Ginger Pye.* Eleanor Estes. (Harcourt Brace Jovanovich)

1953   *Secret of the Andes.* Ann Nolan Clark. (Viking)

1954   *. . . And Now Miguel.* Joseph Krumgold. (T. Y. Crowell)

1955   *The Wheel on the School.* Meindert De Jong. (Harper & Row)

1956   *Carry On, Mr. Bowditch.* Jean Lee Latham. (Houghton Mifflin)

1957   *Miracles on Maple Hill.* Virginia Sorensen. (Harcourt Brace Jovanovich)

1958   *Rifles for Watie.* Harold Keith. (T. Y. Crowell)

1959   *The Witch of Blackbird Pond.* Elizabeth George Speare. (Houghton Mifflin)

1960   *Onion John.* Joseph Krumgold. (T. Y. Crowell)

1961   *Island of the Blue Dolphins.* Scott O'Dell. (Houghton Mifflin)

1962   *The Bronze Bow.* Elizabeth George Speare. (Houghton Mifflin)

1963   *A Wrinkle in Time.* Madeleine L'Engle. (Farrar, Straus & Giroux)

1964   *It's Like This Cat.* Emily Neville. (Harper & Row)

1965   *Shadow of a Bull.* Maia Wojciechowska. (Atheneum)

1966   *I, Jaun de Pareja.* Elizabeth (Borten) de Trevino. (Farrar, Straus & Giroux)

1967   *Up a Road Slowly.* Irene Hunt. (Follett)

1968   *From the Mixed-Up Files of Mrs. Basil E. Frankweiler.* E. L. Konigsburg. (Atheneum)

1969   *The High King.* Lloyd Alexander. (Holt, Rinehart & Winston)

1970   *Sounder.* William Armstrong. (Harper & Row)

1971   *The Summer of the Swans.* Betsy Byars. (Viking)

1972   *Mrs. Frisby and the Rats of Nimh.* Robert O'Brien. (Atheneum)

1973   *Julie of the Wolves.* Jean Craighead George. (Harper)

1974   *The Slave Dancer.* Paula Fox. (Bradbury)

1975   *M. C. Higgins the Great.* Virginia Hamilton. (Macmillan)

1976   *The Grey King.* Susan Cooper. (Atheneum)

1977   *Roll of Thunder, Hear My Cry.* Mildred D. Taylor. (Dial Press)

From *The Teacher's Book of Lists* © 1979, Goodyear Publishing Company, Inc.

CALDECOTT AWARD WINNERS

The first Caldecott Medal, donated by Frederic G. Melcher, was awarded to the artist of the most distinguished American picture book for children published in the United States during the preceding year. The Medal was named for Randolph Caldecott, a famous English illustrator of children's books. The Medal is now donated by Daniel Melcher, son of the original donor.

1938   *Animals of the Bible, a Picture Book.* Illustrated by Dorothy P. Lathrop. Text selected by Helen Dean Fish. (Lippincott)

1939   *Mei Li.* Written and illustrated by Thomas Handforth. (Doubleday)

1940   *Abraham Lincoln.* Written and illustrated by Ingri and Edgar D'Aulaire. (Doubleday)

1941   *They Were Strong and Good.* Written and illustrated by Robert Lawson. (Viking)

1942   *Make Way for Ducklings.* Written and illustrated by Robert McCloskey. (Viking)

1943   *The Little House.* Written and illustrated by Virginia Lee Burton. (Houghton Mifflin)

1944   *Many Moons.* Illustrated by Louis Slobodkin. Written by James Thurber. (Harcourt Brace)

1945   *Prayers for a Child.* Illustrated by Elizabeth Orton Jones. Written by Rachael Field. (Macmillan)

1946   *The Rooster Crows . . .* Illustrated by Maud and Miska Petersham. (Macmillan)

1947   *The Little Island.* Illustrated by Leonard Weisgard. Written by Golden MacDonald. (Doubleday)

1948   *White Snow, Bright Snow.* Illustrated by Roger Duvoisin. Written by Alvin Tresselt. (Lothrop, Lee & Shepard)

1949   *The Big Snow.* Written and illustrated by Berta and Elmer Hader. (Macmillan)

1950   *Song of the Swallows.* Written and illustrated by Leo Politi. (Scribner)

1951   *The Egg Tree.* Written and illustrated by Katherine Milhous. (Scribner)

1952   *Finders Keepers.* Illustrated by Nicolas Mordvinoff. (Harcourt Brace)

1953   *The Biggest Bear.* Written and illustrated by Lynd Ward. (Houghton Mifflin)

1954   *Madeline's Rescue.* Written and illustrated by Ludwig Bemelmans. (Viking)

1955   *Cinderella, or the Little Glass Slipper.* Illustrated and translated from Perrault by Marcia Brown. (Scribner)

1956   *Frog Went A-Courtin'.* Illustrated by Feodor Rojankovsky. (Harcourt Brace Jovanovich)

1957   *A Tree Is Nice.* Illustrated by Marc Simont. Written by Janice May Udry. (Harper & Row)

Wonder. Written and illustrated by Robert McCloskey. (Viking)

...cleer and the Fox. Adapted from Chaucer's *The Canterbury Tales* and illustrated *...*arbara Cooney. (T. Y. Crowell)

1960 *...ne Days to Christmas.* Illustrated by Marie Hall Ets. Written by Marie Hall Ets and Aurora Labastida. (Viking)

1961 *Baroushka and the Three Kings.* Illustrated by Nicolas Sidjakov. Written by Ruth Robbins. (Parnassus)

1962 *Once Upon a Mouse.* Retold and illustrated by Marcia Brown. (Scribner)

1963 *The Snowy Day.* Written and illustrated by Ezra Jack Keats. (Viking)

1964 *Where the Wild Things Are.* Written and illustrated by Maurice Sendak. (Harper & Row)

1965 *May I Bring a Friend?* Illustrated by Beni Montresor. Written by Beatrice Schenk de Regniers. (Atheneum)

1966 *Always Room for One More.* Illustrated by Nonny Hogrogian. Written by Sorche Nic Leodhas. (Holt, Rinehart & Winston)

1967 *Sam, Bangs, and Moonshine.* Written and illustrated by Evaline Ness. (Holt, Rinehart & Winston)

1968 *Drummer Hoff.* Written and illustrated by Ed Emberly. (Prentice-Hall)

1969 *The Fool of the World and the Flying Ship.* Written and illustrated by Arthur Ransome. (Farrar, Straus & Giroux)

1970 *Sylvester and the Magic Pebble.* Written and illustrated by William Steig. (Simon & Schuster)

1971 *A Story, a Story.* Written and illustrated by Gail E. Haley. (Atheneum)

1972 *One Fine Day.* Written and illustrated by Nonny Hogrogrian. (Macmillan)

1973 *The Funny Little Woman.* Illustrated by Blair Lent. Written by Arlene Mosel. (Dutton)

1974 *Duffy and the Devil.* Illustrated by Margot Zemach. Retold by Harve Zemach. (Farrar, Straus & Giroux)

1975 *Arrow to the Sun.* Adapted and illustrated by Gerald McDermott. (Viking)

1976 *Why Mosquitoes Buzz in People's Ears.* Illustrated by Leo and Diane Dillon. Written by Verna Aardema. (Dial)

1977 *Ashanti to Zulu.* Illustrated by Leo and Diane Dillon. Written by Margaret Musgrove. (Dial)

From *The Teacher's Book of Lists* © 1979, Goodyear Publishing Company, Inc.